EssexWorks.
better quality of life

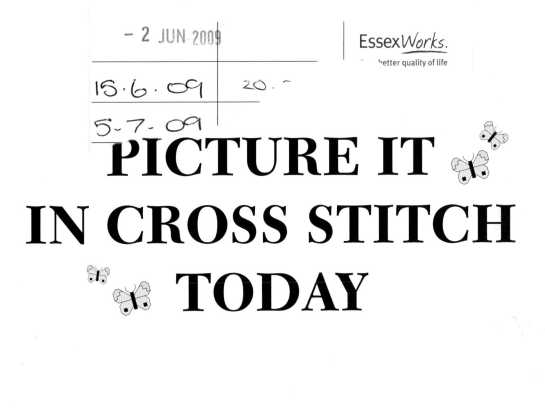

PICTURE IT
IN CROSS STITCH
TODAY

PICTURE IT
IN CROSS STITCH
TODAY

JO VERSO

When this you see remember me
And bear me in your mind;
And be not like the weathercock
That turn att evry wind.
When I am dead and laid in grav
And all my bones are rotten,
By this may I remembered be
When I should be forgotten.
(Sampler 1736)

**Essex County
Council Libraries**

A DAVID & CHARLES BOOK
Copyright © David & Charles Limited 2008

David & Charles is an F+W Publications Inc. company
4700 East Galbraith Road
Cincinnati, OH 45236

First published in the UK in 2008

Text and designs copyright © The Estate of Jo Verso 2008
Layouts, project photography and charts copyright ©
David & Charles 2008

The author's estate and the publisher have made every effort
to ensure that all the instructions in the book are accurate and
safe, and therefore cannot accept liability for any resulting injury,
damage or loss to persons or property, however it may arise.

Names of manufacturers, fabric ranges and other products are
provided for the information of readers, with no intention to
infringe copyright or trademarks.

The publisher would like to thank Linda Clements for her dedicated
attention to detail in the compilation of this new collection, and to
Jo Verso's daughters, Amy and Nancy, for sharing their memories of
their mother, her life and work in the book's introduction.

A catalogue record for this book is available
from the British Library.

ISBN-13: 978-0-7153-2699-2 hardback
ISBN-10: 0-7153-2699-6 hardback

ISBN-13: 978-0-7153-2690-9 paperback
ISBN-10: 0-7153-2690-2 paperback

Printed in China by SNP Leefung Pte Ltd
for David & Charles
Brunel House   Newton Abbot   Devon

Executive Editor Cheryl Brown
Desk Editor Bethany Dymond
Project Editor Lin Clements
Head of Design Prudence Rogers
Charts Ethan Danielson
New Photography Kim Sayer
Jacket Design Stitcher Angela Ottewell
Production Controller Ros Napper

Visit our website at www.davidandcharles.co.uk

David & Charles books are available from all good bookshops;
alternatively you can contact our Orderline on 0870 9908222
or write to us at FREEPOST EX2 110, D&C Direct; Newton Abbot,
TQ12 4ZZ (no stamp required UK only); US customers call
800-289-0963 and Canadian customers call 800-840-5220.

Contents

Foreword

❋·❋·❋·❋·❋·❋·❋·❋·❋·❋·❋·❋✤❋·❋·❋·❋·❋·❋·❋·❋·❋·❋·❋·❋

"I was very honoured to be asked to write this foreword to *Picture It in Cross Stitch Today*. The original book was one of the most innovative cross stitch books ever written and its sound advice, charts and diagrams gave us ordinary mortals the benchmark at which to aim. I was privileged to have known Jo as a friend and I am sure this lovely book will make her new fans all over the world."

I met Jo for the first time when I went to a book signing, just after the publication of *Picture It in Cross Stitch*. I had reason to have mixed feeling about the visit as I knew that we had competed for a book commission and she had won! When I saw her book for the first time, I was so glad I had not made a complete fool of myself and that Jo had done all the hard work. Always a perfectionist, Jo had left nothing to chance and had created something very special, as the extraordinary sales figures went on to prove. There is no doubt that Jo's very distinctive style of design and her extraordinary sense of humour combined to create something very special.

Over the following years, we became firm friends and she could be relied upon to call a spade a shovel when necessary. I can remember being at very low ebb and, at Jo's insistence, was delivered to her house where she suggested she dyed my fringe purple and that we eat jelly with our feet – or try to! This was followed by a trip in her white Porsche, which

she insisted on driving in absurdly high heels, which meant she had to walk back to the house with the aid of a walking stick. Jo had suffered with back problems for many years and I had visited her on many occasions during rough patches. I can remember her preparing coloured charts whilst lying on her side in bed with a three-legged stool bandaged to her legs (it acted as a drawing board) with such determination and humour that it left me feeling very inadequate.

Jo was one of the first designers to champion the use of charting software and she asked me and my husband for dinner and an overnight stay to demonstrate the I.L.Soft programme. She was also responsible for the worst hangover I have ever had – before or since! How I concentrated on the screen the next morning I will never know!

In 1996, The Cross Stitch Guild was founded and we asked Jo to be our Patron, a role I know that she relished. She loved designing, stitching and making things, as her lovely home bore witness to, and she wanted

everyone to feel the same sense of accomplishment she had experienced. The enormous success of *Picture It in Cross Stitch* came as a surprise to her as she was quite unaware of just how clever she was. The book did, and will again, inspire stitchers both new to cross stitch and those of us who knew her work the first time around. It is testament to Jo's talent that *Picture It in Cross Stitch Today* looks as fresh and inviting as its predecessor did 20 years ago and I know that a whole new generation of stitchers will be glad to discover Jo Verso all over again.

Jane Greenoff

Managing Director
The Cross Stitch Guild

This picture captures the essence of *Picture It in Cross Stitch Today* – creating attractive cross stitch pictures unique to you and your family. This charming sampler records Jo's family and life at their house in Greville Road in Kenilworth. To see how easy it is to design your own sampler, turn to pages 22–23.

A Life in Stitches

It is a great pleasure for us to introduce this new edition of *Picture It in Cross Stitch*, two decades after its first publication. Twenty years ago, at 14 and 10 years old respectively, we had little idea of the impact that our mother's work would have, and the enormous fan base she would build up over the course of her exceptional though tragically short career.

From a young age cross stitch was a major factor in our lives, with every significant milestone dutifully recorded by our proud mother in her own distinctive style. Her fans – many of whom we have had the pleasure of meeting – have told us that they felt they knew both Jo and her family personally, as they shared, through her writing and embroidery, so many of the special moments in our lives.

The legacy that our mother has left behind is a constant source of joy to both of us, and many of our cherished memories of her relate to the years she spent perfecting her art form. During the summers when a book was in progress, our father would take us away on holidays, leaving Jo in the peace of her attic workroom to design – translating her rare wit into stitches, which will continue to enchant and amuse us long into the future.

Before the days of computer charting, Jo would diligently design using graph paper coloured in with sticky plastic overlay, expertly cut to size for every shape. Leftover pieces would be stuck on the edge of the drawing board, but would inevitably end up attached to her sleeves

Jo had a clear creative streak from a very young age. Here, aged three, she is clearly deep in concentration at her painting – no one could have predicted what an artist she would become.

Jo as a '60s mod during her university days in Dublin. It was here she met her first husband, and the girls' father, Robin.

JO VERSO'S **CROSS STITCH YEAR**
JO VERSO'S COMPLETE CROSS STITCH COURSE
Jo Verso CROSS STITCH GIFTS FOR CHILDREN
Jo Verso WORLD OF CROSS STITCH
Jo Verso CROSS STITCH CARDS & KEEPSAKES
Jo Verso PICTURE IT IN CROSS STITCH

Jo Verso's bookshelf

• *Picture It in Cross Stitch* September 1988
314,774 copies sold

• *Cross Stitch Cards & Keepsakes* September 1990
232,315 copies sold

• *World of Cross Stitch* September 1992
167,304 copies sold

• *Cross Stitch Gifts for Children* March 1995
51,344 copies sold

• *Jo Verso's Complete Cross Stitch Course* August 1996
77,741 copies sold

• *Jo Verso's Cross Stitch Year* June 1998
60,320 copies sold

'My Cross Stitch Year' depicting Jo and her second husband Malcolm, Nancy and Amy, Malcolm's children Phil and Wanda, and assorted pets, taken from *Jo Verso's Cross Stitch Year*.

and transferred to other parts of her life. We will never forget those distinctive 'chewy bits' that would turn up in the sandwiches unwrapped at school, or in the casserole she had prepared for our evening meal. When the team at David & Charles announced to her that they would be marketing her as the 'Delia Smith of Cross Stitch', she corrected them by saying, to the contrary, that 'Delia Smith is the Jo Verso of Cookery' – although we have

yet to find this 'secret ingredient' in any of Delia's recipes!

Both of us have picked up a needle and thread at various points and contributed to the stitching in our mother's numerous books. One whole summer was spent in endless stitching, one of us with a leg in plaster, and winter evenings were often whiled away with the three of us stitching against the clock for the next looming deadline.

(Below) Jo's book signings attracted huge numbers of fans, with queues usually snaking out of the door, all eager for a chance to meet her in person.

(Above) Jo's attic workroom was a hive of creativity, with inspiring pictures on the walls and drawers bursting with threads, beads, buttons and charms.
(Right) A proud Jo stands in front of the window display of her local Blackwells branch for the launch of *Picture It in Cross Stitch* in 1988.

(Below) Amy's third birthday in 1981 – despite her deadlines, Jo always made time for a homemade birthday cake.

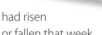

(Above) Amy's christening at St Austin's Church in Kenilworth in 1978. Naturally, the event was commemorated in cross stitch (see page 91).

(Above) Summer 1975 – Jo and baby Nancy smile for the camera.

On completion of every book, she would make the trip down to Newton Abbot in Devon to deliver the text and artworks, and return home elated. On publication, the parties were legendary. Just before shaking hands on each new contract, at the final moment she would ask for a case of champagne for the launch, smuggle several bottles home for our own private enjoyment, and scenes of much hilarity would ensue.

That teenage syndrome of being terminally embarrassed by one's parents rang particularly true for us. Imagine how mortifying it was for us to pass the local bookshop and see the whole window dedicated to our mother, in the knowledge that all our friends would see it. In truth, the embarrassment was entirely feigned – we were, of course, inordinately proud, and when *Picture It in Cross Stitch*, her first published work, became a bestseller, would try to snatch the newspaper from each other to be the first to read the top-ten list and see if it had risen or fallen that week.

Above all, it was Jo's sense of humour that both we and her fans hold most dear. Her extraordinary personality and charm shone through in everything she created. When brainstorming the title of what was to become *Picture It in Cross Stitch*, her personal favourite was *Cross Stitch Your*

(Left) Nancy's 18th birthday display case and Amy's room door plate from *Cross Stitch Gifts for Children*.
(Centre) Nancy and Amy on a family summer holiday in Ireland, 1983. Later, Jo often stayed at home to work on her books.
(Right) Both the girls attended Kenilworth School, and their teachers were immortalized in *World of Cross Stitch*.

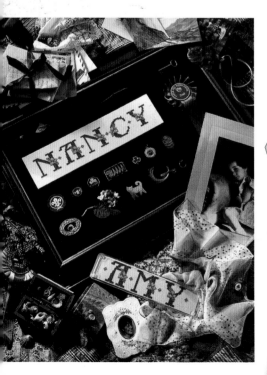

(Left) The girls share Christmas with their teddies under the tree, 1986. Jo adored Christmas and always went to great efforts to decorate the house, book deadline or not!

(Right) Clinton School's nativity play in 1983 featured a nervous young Amy as a shepherd (front right). Events like these fired Jo's creative imagination.

Amy's Christmas stocking from *Cross Stitch Gifts for Children*.

(Above) Jo unwraps the sandwiches at a family picnic in 1980, with Amy aged two and Nancy aged six.
(Centre) Nancy was a keen ballet dancer from a young age – another 'milestone' that was recorded in cross stitch in *Cross Stitch Gifts for Children*.
(Right) Nancy's 'Milestones' picture.

Guinea Pig, a title that, understandably, never made it past the marketing team. Her 'signature' – a butterfly incorporated into many of her samplers – captured perfectly her incredible lightness of being, but also her ultimate fragility. Her loss will be felt for a generation.

Since her death in a road accident in France in 2002, both of our lives have gone on, as they inevitably do. We are both married now, and Jo has recently become a grandmother. That these events will never be recorded in cross stitch – as all those other rites of passage were – is a source of great sorrow to us, as we know that she would have taken such delight in chronicling these in her own unique way. However, we also take enormous comfort and delight in the fact that her memory

lives on through her work, and a new generation of cross stitchers will be inspired by her designs through this wonderful new edition, which is a real tribute and celebration of her tremendous talent.

We hope that you gain as much enjoyment from these pages as those that read them 20 years ago, and that you will be inspired to create wonderful samplers of your own family, so that they too will have such memories to cherish in their own futures, as we have in ours.

Nancy and Amy Verso

(Above) Jo and Malcolm on their wedding day in the Florida Keys in 1997 with their best friends Roy and Elia.

Introduction

In 1978, shortly before the birth of my second daughter, the last few stitches were completed in a patch-work bedspread that had been four years in the making. Standing back to view the result it was obvious that the finishing touch to the room would be an old-fashioned cross stitch sampler to hang on the wall over the bed. The search for such a sampler led to an absorbing hobby, a new job, and eventually to writing this book.

My hunt for a sampler led me first to the local antique shops. Here it became obvious that because samplers were embroidered on linen, using many coloured threads, they have proved to be decorative and durable documents. Equally, their survival is due to the personal nature of these documents incorporating, as they do, details of family life among their borders and alphabets. This personal quality has saved many samplers from being discarded or sold, so the few that find their way into antique shops are collectors' items and command high prices beyond my pocket. Reluctantly I decided to stitch my own sampler.

The next port of call was the local needlecraft shop to buy a kit. Having embroidered nothing more than a tray-cloth at school, it was a relief to see that the main stitch used was cross stitch, one of the easiest stitches to produce with good results. Disappointingly, the kits offered little scope for personalization other than a few names and dates. What had so appealed about the old samplers was the glimpse they gave into life as it was lived at the time they were sewn. The idea of leaving a picture of my own life to future generations of my family was beginning to appeal to me.

If the decision to stitch my own sampler was taken reluctantly, the prospect of designing it as well was even more daunting. My final destination was the local stationers where a stock of graph paper was bought. Not being an artist, consolation was taken from the observation that cross stitch patterns tend to be more stylized than naturalistic, and there were pattern books from which motifs could be copied. By selectively choosing many bits and pieces out of several books, and making generous use of an eraser, my own design was produced (see opposite). The result hung over the bed for many years, complete with all its beginner's mistakes. Along with the traditional border, alphabet, numbers and motifs, it portrays my own house, the cat and my family, including the baby, who by the time of sewing had arrived and was represented in her pram. Also included was a motto of my own choice, and all this was sewn in a colour scheme to match the bedspread that had given rise to the whole undertaking. The biggest surprise was how a daunting chore turned out to be immensely enjoyable, and the satisfaction derived from stitching my own family proved to be addictive.

I have since created many samplers, pictures, cards and other documents for my family and friends. Hopefully, these will be of interest not only to future generations of our family, but also to needleworkers and social historians.

This 20th Anniversary Edition

This book is a celebration of the work of Jo Verso, bringing this, her first and most successful title, back into print in an extended 20th anniversary edition. The book has been revised to include modern materials and ideas but the aim of the book remains the same – to give cross stitchers the techniques to enable them to create and stitch designs that celebrate *their* families, *their* homes and *their* stories.

Some of the designs can be sewn straight off the page but most are designed as a basic pattern, with instructions on how to change them to suit your circumstances. Photographs show how the basic pattern has been adapted; all you have to do is study the differences and make your own changes.

The charts in this new edition are in colour to give you a good idea of how the finished embroidery will look. The charts within the chapters have keys giving the colours used but you can easily change the colours to suit you. The extensive Motif Library on pages 100–142 has hundreds of motifs that can be used and adapted to your life or to that of your friends, inspiring you to try your hand at designing. These charts are also in colour but the specific colours you use are up to you, so no keys are included.

In these days of mass production, handmade embroidery is to be prized. People still love to record details of their lives and the extensive advice in this book is as relevant now as it ever was.

Designing the Charts

To produce your own, personalized cross stitch picture, be it a greetings card or a sampler, you will need a chart to serve as a pattern from which you will work the stitches. Charts in this book are intended to be used as a basis to which you can add your own personal touches and details.

Materials and Equipment

To adapt a chart you will need to copy and make changes to the basic charts, and you should therefore equip yourself with the following materials and equipment.

Graph Paper

Cross stitch patterns are drawn on to graph paper and then translated into stitches by counting the squares on the chart – each filled square equals one full cross stitch on the fabric (see Fig 1). Graph paper can be bought as sheets, by the roll, or in pads. Small sheets can be glued together to form larger ones, taking care to line up the squares accurately at the join. A graph paper with ten squares to 1in (2.5cm) is probably best: the squares aren't so small that you strain your eyes whilst drawing them, nor so large that the finished chart is unwieldy to use as a sewing pattern. You will need a sheet large enough for the finished design, called a master sheet, and spare graph paper for drawing the different 'ingredients' of your design, which could be motifs, symbols, figures or lettering.

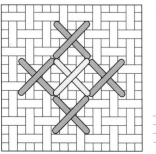

Fig 1 One full square on the chart becomes one full cross stitch on the fabric

Lead Pencil, Sharpener and Eraser

Not all pencils are a pleasure to use, so experiment with a few types until you find one that suits you. Choose one with a lead that is soft enough to erase easily, but not so soft that it smudges – try an HB or a B. A propelling pencil is useful as it does not need frequent sharpening.

A sharp pencil line is important when drawing on the graph paper to produce an accurate pattern. A craft knife is an excellent choice for sharpening, especially for crayons that persist in breaking in an ordinary sharpener.

Use a good quality eraser – the type that slips on to the end of a pencil ensures that your eraser is always to hand when it is needed.

Coloured Crayons

If you colour in your chart with the approximate colours you intend to use, when you come to sew the design you will have a fair indication of how the finished result will look. A colour chart is easier to follow at the sewing stage than a black and white chart, which uses symbols to indicate colour changes. However, no range of crayons can match the enormous number of coloured threads that are available, so be content to give a general

guide. More subtle decisions about colour can be made later when the threads and fabric are chosen.

Tracing Paper

If you are unable to find the design you require, ready charted in a book for you to copy, do not be daunted at the prospect of producing your own – tracing paper will come to the rescue. Anything that you cannot draw can be traced from a book, or other source, and can be transferred to the graph paper where it is squared up to produce an embroidery pattern (see Squaring Up an Image on page 18). Greaseproof paper will do at a pinch, but real tracing paper, available at good stationers, is superior in every respect. You may be able to find graphed tracing paper, which has a graph grid printed on to it. This is laid over the design, which is then traced on to the squares (Fig 2 overleaf), ready for squaring up. Alternatively, draw a grid on computer and print the grid on to plain tracing paper.

Photocopiers can copy a sheet of graph paper on to transparent acetate sheets, such as are used in overhead projectors. This transparent sheet can then be laid over an illustration and the pattern is at once clearly visible, in colour, through the grid on the sheet. It can then be copied straight on to graph paper.

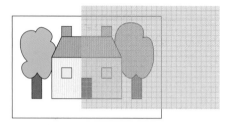

Fig 2 Graphed tracing paper laid over an illustration

Scissors

Paper-cutting scissors are needed to cut out your cross stitch motifs for arrangement on the master sheet. Do not be tempted to use your sharp embroidery scissors on paper as you will blunt them.

Adhesive

You will need adhesive to fix your motifs to the master sheet once you have decided on their final position. Adhesive is also needed to stick small sheets of graph paper together to make larger ones. Sticky tape is not suitable. Use an adhesive that will not wet and distort the paper, making it difficult to align the squares on the graph paper. If you are the decisive type and trust your own judgement you can use a glue that, once applied, does not allow for repositioning – a solid glue that comes in stick form is ideal. If you use cow gum you can change your mind, even weeks later, over the positioning of a design. Once dry, you can (with care) peel the paper off without tearing or marking the master sheet, and with another application of gum you can try again. There are also spray adhesives used for mounting photographs and art work; this has the advantage that one spray allows you to peel and re-stick several times before another application is necessary.

Light Source

Tracing is made easier if a light is placed behind the work in progress. The most readily available source of light during daylight hours is at a window, and this is adequate for most needs. The work to be traced is positioned behind the tracing paper and is then held up against the glass. However, holding this position for any length of time is guaranteed to make your arms ache. If you are going to do a lot of tracing, it would be best to buy a simple light box.

tip

Re-sealable or zip-top plastic bags are useful for keeping items of equipment in, and also for housing the finished, cut-out motifs.

COMPUTER CHARTING

Many people now use software programs to produce cross stitch designs, and there are many packages available. Most also have large libraries of images that you can use. How you use charting software depends on you: some people like to design straight on to the screen; some like to draw their images as described in the following pages and then scan or copy these drawings into the computer; others create designs using traditional media, such as paint, and then scan the image into the computer, to be re-interpreted in cross stitch. There are various advantages to using charting software:

- The images created can be manipulated in lots of interesting and time-saving ways – they can be copied and pasted, flipped, rotated, reduced and enlarged – all with the click of a mouse.

- Borders are easily created, including right-angled corners, using the copying and rotating functions.

- The colours you use can be easily changed, allowing you to experiment with the overall colour balance of a design. Full colour palettes of the main thread manufacturers are usually available.

- Most programs have a range of stitches available and often facilities to design your own stitches. Beads can also be charted.

- Some programs allow you to print the design in a fabric format, which is useful as it enables you to see what the finished design might look like once stitched.

- Charts can be saved in different formats and can easily be emailed to a friend or cross stitch magazine.

Sources of Design Material

Throughout this book you will find patterns that may be suitable for the design you want to create and from pages 100–142 there is an extensive Motif Library with hundreds of useful motifs on a wide range of subjects.

tip

Computer software packages used to create posters, greetings cards, personalized stationery and so on, often have large libraries of images you can copy and adapt to cross stitch motifs.

- There are many other cross stitch pattern books on the market, in which you may find just the designs you want, or you may be able to put together your own chart using a pattern from one book together with patterns from others. Take care that designs you use are copyright free and that you only use commercial designs for personal use.

- If you cannot find what you want in an existing pattern book, you may find something that you can adapt and alter to produce the design you want. If all else fails, you will have to make your own design. If you doubt your ability to draw, use tracing paper and find pictures to trace of those things you want to depict.

- An invaluable source of material is your local library, particularly the children's section. Illustrations in children's reference books tend to be simplified line drawings, which automatically make easier your task of tracing and squaring up. Books for babies are particularly good for simplified shapes of animals and everyday objects.

- Reference books and catalogues usually have pictures of whatever it is you feel unable to draw.

- If you are working on a design of your house, you will find it useful to work from a photograph of it. If you do not have access to a camera, you will need to make a rough sketch (see page 56).

- If you want to depict a building that is a local landmark you may be able to work from a postcard.

- Wedding photographs are useful if you want details of the church, and the appearance of the participants, to be accurate in a wedding design.

- If you have access to the Internet use one of the search engines to look for images you need (remembering to respect copyright). There are thousands of images that can be adapted and used as cross stitch motifs

Drawing Your Illustrations

Whether you are designing a large picture or a small decorated initial, first make a list of everything to include in your design. Each item can then be drawn out on to separate pieces of graph paper. When all items on the list have been drawn, excess graph paper is trimmed, ready to arrange them on to a large master sheet of graph paper. This allows you to try different layouts before deciding on the most pleasing, and saves erasing and re-drawing.

Copying Directly on to Graph Paper

If the items on your list can be found in existing pattern books and you are happy that they do not need to be changed in any way, they can simply be copied directly from the book on to your graph paper. Take care to copy accurately. If the pattern is printed using key symbols to denote colour changes, you may find it easier to colour your chart in with crayons, then when you come to sew it, you will see at a glance which colour you should be using.

If the pattern in the book needs a change or two of detail to make it more suitable, copy it out as before and erase those areas you want to change. Add the new details you require (see also Fig 1 on page 58).

Tracing an Illustration on to Graph Paper

If the items on your list cannot be found ready charted, you will have to make your own chart, but if you are not artistic there is no need to panic; anything that you feel you cannot draw can be traced from books or other sources. Trace the illustration on to tracing paper, and then transfer it on to graph paper. If you are using graphed tracing paper, line up as many vertical and horizontal lines as possible before you start to trace your illustration as this will make the job of squaring up easier.

Frequently the illustration of the object you wish to include in your embroidery will be the wrong size, so before you trace it on to the graph paper it will need to be reduced or enlarged as the case might be.

Squaring Up an Image

Whether you have drawn your illustration directly on to the graph paper or have used tracing paper, it will now need squaring up to turn it into a pattern for cross stitch embroidery.

At this stage you will probably have a drawing with flowing, curved lines (Fig 3a below), but in a cross stitch pattern one full square is translated into one full cross stitch, so all curves must be eliminated, leaving only complete squares.

Take your pencil and draw over the lines of your illustration on the graph paper. Follow the original drawing as closely as possible, but never let the pencil stray away from the graph lines. Where the original line starts to climb upwards, bring the pencil line up one square; when it dips, come down one square. Follow the original line all the way round the design; your original flowing shape will now look more angular (Fig 3b).

Now erase the original line of the illustration, leaving the new, squared-up pattern ready to be coloured in (Fig 3c).

Q: How do I reduce or enlarge an image?

Once your image is the right size it can be traced on to graph paper ready to be squared up into a pattern. You can use a photocopier for reducing and enlarging images to the size required. These are available in many libraries or in stationers. Many people have access to flat-bed scanners, which allow an image to be scanned into a computer and then scaled up or down to the size needed.

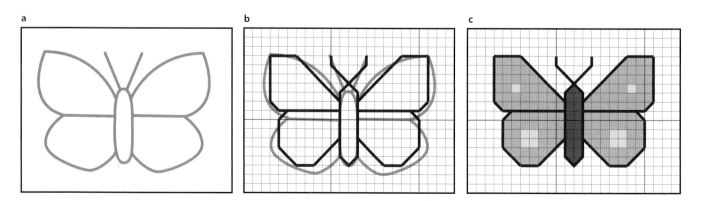

Fig 3 Squaring up an image: a) draw or trace an image on to graph paper; b) square up the image; c) colour the chart ready for use

It is important to stay exactly on the lines of the graph paper; pencil lines that stray randomly into the spaces may make your drawing look better and more natural, but the pattern will be unsewable (Fig 4).

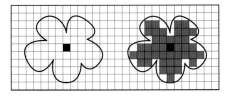

Fig 4 The first motif here cannot be sewn in full cross stitch; only the red areas shown on the second motif can be sewn in full cross stitch

You will notice that curved lines have been translated into a series of 'steps', because the pattern is now made of squares. This angularity presents some difficulties in the designing of small things with subtle, curving lines. Anything can be charted for cross stitch providing you are prepared to work on a larger scale; the more squares you have to play with, i.e., the larger the finished design, the more natural and realistic the result can be. So if, after squaring up, the design of your pet mouse looks more like a dented matchbox with whiskers (Fig 5), there are two ways to get a better result. You can make your design larger and allow more squares to achieve a better shape (but its proportions by now will be elephantine, as the second mouse shows) or, if 'small is beautiful', design it using three-quarter cross stitch in addition to full cross stitch.

Achieving Realism and Adding Details

The use of three-quarter cross stitch enables you to achieve more realism in a small design, while the inclusion of backstitch and French knots allows details to be included that make a design more recognisable. Off-setting cross stitches also helps you achieve a more realistic look to some motifs.

Three-quarter Cross Stitch

If a full cross stitch forms a square shape when it is sewn, then a three-quarter cross stitch forms the shape of a right-angled triangle (Fig 6). If squares and right-angled triangles are combined in a design it is easier to suggest subtle shapes, and the eye can be fooled into thinking it sees curves and circles.

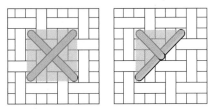

Fig 6 A full cross stitch forms a square shape when sewn (shown here on evenweave fabric); a three-quarter cross stitch forms a right-angled triangle

A more recognisable mouse can now be charted on a smaller scale more befitting its size (Fig 7). Accuracy is still important; with three-quarter cross stitch the pencil line must bisect the square exactly from corner to corner – there is no such thing as one-third cross stitch. So make sure your pencil line on the chart stays on the graph lines, or where you want to indicate the use of a three-quarter cross stitch; it must go diagonally across the square to form a right-angled triangle.

Even with the added possibilities afforded by the use of three-quarter cross stitch, complete accuracy and realism are not possible, nor are they desirable in this medium. Your design will be an *interpretation* of the event or subject

you are portraying: if faithful accuracy is essential, hang a photograph on the wall instead. Allow yourself some artistic licence – include as much detail as you can to make your subject recognisable without cluttering your design unnecessarily.

Backstitch

The use of backstitch and French knots allows the addition of small details to your cross stitch, turning a meaningless design into an instantly recognisable one (Fig 8).

Backstitch is most often used to outline something that would otherwise be indistinguishable from the background or from other areas of stitching. For example, a white house stitched on to white linen would be hard to see without outlining the side walls in a darker colour. Backstitch is also used where something needs to be emphasized, or for small details like mouths and so on. It is invaluable for lettering where there isn't enough space to allow the use of a cross stitch alphabet.

The use of backstitch is indicated on a chart by a solid line. Every motif in this book has been outlined because you may choose to work the design in pale colours, which require backstitching. If, however, the contrasts between colours are sufficient when you have sewn your designs you may not need to backstitch, so you can only outline where you feel it's necessary. Backstitch can break the rules about straying off the lines of the graph paper, and can make use of any holes in the fabric covered by the design.

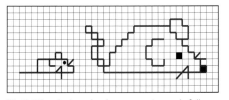

Fig 5 Mice designed to be sewn using only full cross stitches – not the most realistic!

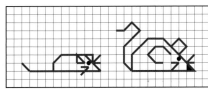

Fig 7 Mice designed to be sewn using three-quarter cross stitch in addition to full cross stitch

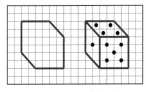

Fig 8 The addition of details sewn in backstitch and French knots can make all the difference

French Knots

French knots are invaluable for indicating eyes, buttons, badges, beads, musical notes and numerous other small details on a design. They can appear singly, as in the case of eyes, or they can be grouped together in clusters to form bouquets of flowers, raspberries and so on. They are indicated on charts by a small coloured circle or a knot shape.

OFF-SETTING

This is a useful technique where a line rises neither vertically nor at an obliging angle of 45°, for example a church steeple. As the line rises, rows of cross stitches can be placed half a square across on the chart, rather than a full square. At the sewing stage the off-set stitches are sewn one thread to the right or left of the previous stitching. Where more than one full cross stitch is involved, take care to off-set the whole row, not leaving a half stitch at the end of the row, which will be unsewable. Note: some charting software packages do not allow cross stitches to be offset.

Fig 9 The diagram shows the top two cross stitches off-set by one thread on the fabric (half a square on the chart). The fireman's helmet charted here has the single cross stitch at the top off-set.

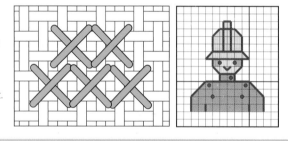

Lettering

Draw out alphabets or words on to long strips of graph paper, which can then be cut to size later to fit the design. Do not worry too much about the spacing between letters and words; if you make a mistake simply cut the strip at the appropriate place and overlap to make the space smaller, or insert more paper to expand the word. This is generally quicker than erasing and re-drawing the lettering.

There are no hard and fast rules about how many spaces to leave between letters and lines as alphabets vary so much in style and size. Draw out your lettering, look at it from a distance and trust your eye to tell you where you have gone wrong; it is then a simple matter to cut and make adjustments to the spacing.

To centre a strip of lettering on to your design, fold the strip to find the centre and line up this point with the central line of your design, thus avoiding a lot of counting. Lettering can be worked either in cross stitch or, where space is limited, in backstitch. See page 46 for easy steps to charting your own text.

Q: How do I design an embroidery to fit an existing frame?

If you are designing an embroidery to fit an existing frame (or piece of fabric) you will have to do some maths to determine the maximum size of the piece of graph paper on to which you will fit all your design material (your master sheet). If, however, you plan to have a frame made for the embroidery when it is completed, your master sheet can be of any size you choose.

1 Measure the space inside the frame. Allow for a mount if you plan to use one, and decide on the size of the space you wish to fill with the design. (If you are working in centimetres, 2.5cm = 1 inch.)
2 If working on Aida fabric, count how many *blocks* there are to 1in (2.5cm) and you will get the number of cross stitches that will be worked on 1in of the fabric (cross stitches are generally worked over *one* block of Aida).
3 Multiply the number of available inches by the number of crosses per inch to get the size of your master sheet. For example, if the space to be filled with embroidery measures 6 x 4in and the thread count is 10 cross stitches to 1in, multiply 6 x 10 = 60 and 4 x 10 = 40. Your master sheet, and consequently your finished design, must measure no more than 60 x 40 squares if the embroidery is to fit the frame (see Fig 10).

If working on evenweave fabric, count how many *threads* there are to 1in (2.5cm) and you will get the number of cross stitches that will be worked on 1in of the fabric. As evenweave is usually worked over *two* threads, divide this number by two to give you the number of cross stitches per inch, and then calculate the size of the finished design as in step 3.

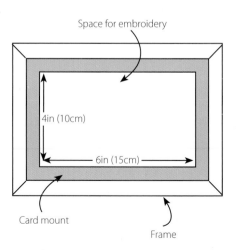

Fig 10 Measuring a frame to calculate the overall size of the master sheet

Space for embroidery

4in (10cm)

6in (15cm)

Card mount

Frame

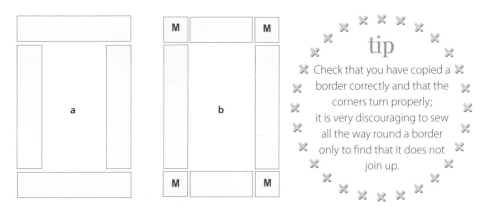

Borders

A border is often necessary to provide a 'frame' for all the separate elements you have included in your design. The simplest border of all can be a single retaining line. Small designs generally look better with a narrow border, but with larger pieces of work you can be more ambitious.

Draw out your border on to four long strips of graph paper to the approximate size you think you will need (Fig 11a). To enlarge a border later, to fit around your design, add extra pattern repeats. To make it smaller, cut the strips and remove the necessary number of repeats.

Borders can also be formed using one or more bands, with or without a symbol in each corner (Fig 11b). Where a pattern repeat slopes markedly in one direction, it may be desirable to break the run at the centre of each side and reverse the pattern at this point to ensure four similar corners (Fig 12 and Fig 13). Borders can also have corners created so they are continuous – see below.

When you have drawn out your border, ask yourself if it would benefit from the addition of an inner and outer retaining line. A variety of borders and corners is shown on pages 134–137 of the Motif Library.

Fig 11 Placement of bands (a) or bands plus corner motifs (M) to form borders (b)

tip
Check that you have copied a border correctly and that the corners turn properly; it is very discouraging to sew all the way round a border only to find that it does not join up.

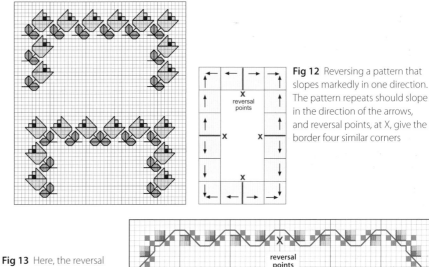

Fig 12 Reversing a pattern that slopes markedly in one direction. The pattern repeats should slope in the direction of the arrows, and reversal points, at X, give the border four similar corners

Fig 13 Here, the reversal point (X) shows where a border is flipped, mirroring the original design

Q: How do I create a border corner?

If you choose a band as a basis for a continuous border (such as one of those in the Motif Library), you will need to invent a corner. The simplest way to do this is with a small hand mirror. Place the mirror on your band at an angle of 45º and move it along the band until a pleasing corner is reflected in the mirror. It is then a simple matter to draw out the new corner (Fig 14).

Alternatively you could scan the band into a computer, then copy the design, paste it, rotate it 90º and position it against the original horizontal border.

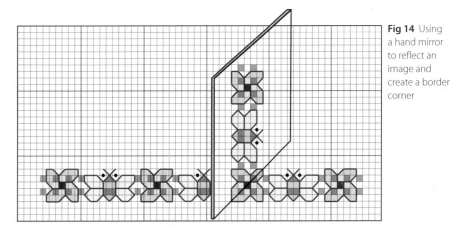

Fig 14 Using a hand mirror to reflect an image and create a border corner

Designing a Sampler – in a nutshell. . .

All of the information given so far has been distilled here into four steps, so you can refer to these pages and quickly refresh your memory before starting a project. See pages 56–59 for more detailed advice on designing a house and family sampler.

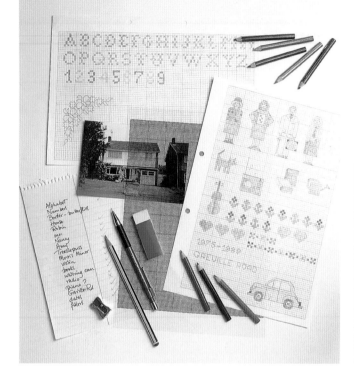

Step 1

Make a list of everything you would like to include in your sampler. When designing the sampler on page 7, my list read as follows: a butterfly border; an alphabet; numbers; my house; myself; my husband Robin; my daughters Nancy and Amy; the cat; my Morris Minor car; Nancy's music; Amy's violin; my two books; my husband's interest in gardening (a watering can); hearts and flowers to fill any gaps (fillers); locations and dates.

Copy out each design on the list on to graph paper in pencil. Colour in each design with coloured crayons and then cut out each one with paper-cutting scissors, leaving one clear square all round.

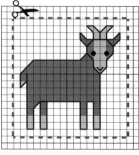

Fig 15 Cutting out a motif

Step 2

When all the motifs have been copied, coloured and cut out, lay them on to the master sheet and begin to build up the design, shuffling them around until you achieve a pleasing, balanced design. Because you have not drawn directly on to the master sheet, you can try out many different combinations without having to erase and re-draw every time you change your mind. This saves a lot of time and irritation.

tip
Store all the motifs in an envelope to prevent them getting lost or ending up in the vacuum cleaner!

tip
When cutting out motifs, don't cut along the drawing line as this will be far too fiddly: cut the design out as a rectangle or square, leaving a minimum of one clear square all round (Fig 15).

tip
Be flexible when arranging the drawings on to the master sheet. If a particular item will not fit or is out of character with the rest, it may be better to put it aside for use on another occasion rather than squeeze it in and spoil your design.

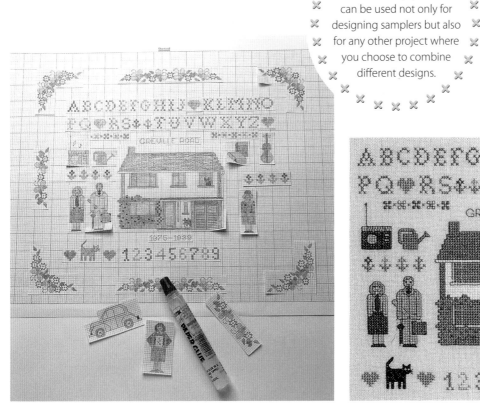

tip

This four-step process can be used not only for designing samplers but also for any other project where you choose to combine different designs.

Step 3

When you are satisfied with the arrangement of all the slips, stick them to the master sheet using a non-permanent adhesive, as this will allow you to reposition the slips several times. Take care to align the squares on the slips with the lines on the master sheet. Pin your finished design up in a room where you will see it frequently. If anything needs to be moved or changed it will soon become obvious.

Step 4

When satisfied with your design, draw it out again on to another master sheet, which will then be your pattern for stitching. If you work from the first master sheet, the non-permanent glue might allow motifs to come adrift during stitching. To save time, you could colour photocopy the first master sheet. You are now ready to start stitching!

DESIGNING ON COMPUTER

If you are preparing a chart using computing software, the four stages described above still apply, except that you will probably be charting your motifs 'on screen', or pasting them on to the screen from a library of images.

Once you have all the motifs and elements on the list made in Step 1, instead of sticking them on to a master sheet you will be able to select each element and move it around on screen to the position you want. The advantage of computer charting this way means that you can print out versions of the design at any stage and decide which you like best.

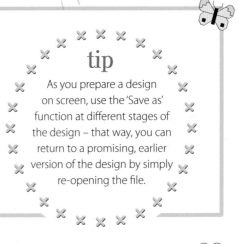

tip

As you prepare a design on screen, use the 'Save as' function at different stages of the design – that way, you can return to a promising, earlier version of the design by simply re-opening the file.

Preparing to Sew

Whilst your charted 'masterpiece' is pinned on the wall to see if it still meets with your approval after a week, use the time to acquire the materials you will need to sew it. These will include embroidery fabric and threads and small pieces of equipment, such as needles, scissors and embroidery hoops – see below for advice.

Fabrics

Fabrics for counted cross stitch must have an even weave, with the same number of weft (horizontal) threads as there are warp (vertical) threads to 1in (2.5cm). If the fabric is not evenweave, the designs will be distorted in the sewing. Suitable evenweave fabrics can be either linen or cotton. The latter is cheaper but whatever the fabric make sure you choose a thread count or gauge (see below) that will not strain your eyes. You will need a piece of fabric large enough to accommodate your sewn design, with enough spare fabric all round the edges to allow 5–8cm (2–3in) for turnings to be made when the finished embroidery is mounted and framed (see below).

Evenweave Linen

This fabric is woven with single threads (so is called single weave) and has excellent qualities of durability and handling, which are reflected in its price. It is available in many colours from various manufacturers and can be bought by the yard or metre and also as small off-cuts and mixed packs of smaller pieces. Evenweave linen is available in a variety of thread counts – a thread count being the number of threads there are to 1in (2.5cm). The smaller the number of such threads, the larger the weave is, and the larger will be the cross stitch that is worked on it. Conversely, the higher the number of threads to 1in (2.5cm), the finer the fabric, and the smaller the cross stitches will be. As evenweave linen is made from natural linen fibres, some of the threads are coarser than others, and so the cross stitch is worked over two threads to even out any discrepancies. Thus, an evenweave linen with a thread count of 28 threads to 1in (2.5cm) will produce 14 cross stitches to 1in (2.5cm).

Aida Fabric

This cotton fabric is woven to form a block of threads between each hole, and the cross stitch is worked over one block. Various colours and counts, including 18, 14 and 11 blocks to 1in (2.5cm) are available. This fabric is not ideal for a design with lots of three-quarter cross stitches, as there is no hole to accommodate the quarter stitch that is made over the half cross stitch. It is possible though to pierce a hole for the quarter stitch in the centre of the block of threads, using a sharp needle.

Hardanger Fabric

This is a cotton fabric available in many colours. It is not a single-weave fabric but is woven with pairs of threads, which give a denser background than a linen of the same thread count. The holes between the pairs of threads are easy to see and the count is usually 22 pairs of threads to 1in (2.5cm). When a cross stitch is worked over two pairs of threads, this fabric will produce 11 cross stitches to 1in (2.5cm).

Q: How much fabric do I buy?

If your eyes glaze over at the mention of maths, be warned – mistakes in fabric shops can be expensive (see overleaf).

1 Count the number of stitches across the height of the design and then the width – this is the stitch count.

2 Divide each of these numbers by the fabric count number, e.g., 140 stitches x 140 stitches ÷ by a 14-count Aida = a finished design size of 10 x 10in (25.5 x 25.5cm). (Working on evenweave usually means working over two threads, so divide the fabric count by two before you start.)

3 Round figures up to the nearest 1cm (½in), erring on the generous side and add on a making up or turning allowance of 7.5cm (3in) on each side. So, for an embroidery with a finished size of 25.5 x 25.5cm (10 x 10in) you will need a piece of fabric 40.5 x 40.5cm (16 x 16in).

If you already have a piece of fabric and would like to design an embroidery to fit it see page 20 (designing an embroidery to fit an existing frame).

BUYING FABRIC

A little fabric know-how will help prevent costly fabric-buying mistakes and make the best use of the fabric you do buy.

- Fabric can be expensive, especially if bought by the width, so either share with friends, or buy the smaller off-cuts that many fabric shops have available. Fabric manufacturers now provide pre-cut pieces of fabric in a range of different sizes.

- Before buying your fabric, check it for flaws. Sometimes a flaw can be covered by embroidery or can be lost in a turning, but do inspect the fabric carefully before it is cut from the roll.

- Check for dirty marks, particularly along creases, as it is better not to have to wash the fabric before you embroider it.

- When you buy your fabric, ensure that the assistant cuts the fabric carefully along a thread line. If not, you will have to pull a thread out and cut again to straighten it, which is irritating and wasteful.

- When cutting a large piece of fabric into smaller pieces always cut along a thread line and aim, if possible, to have the selvedge edge at the side edges of the embroidery.

Preparing Fabric

Taking the time to prepare your embroidery fabric before you begin to stitch will save time in the long run, and help you to produce neater work.

1 Cut the fabric to the size you require or the size stated in the project instructions. When working designs from other books or magazines and no size is stated, you must ensure that you have allowed enough fabric for the design (see previous page). When cutting fabric do use sharp dressmaking scissors and do not be tempted to use your embroidery scissors – these should only be used to cut embroidery thread. If possible, make a note of where the selvedges are on the fabric piece and aim to have these on the left and right of the design as it is stitched as this will make the stretching of the finished piece a little easier.

2 Oversew the edges of the fabric to prevent fraying: this can be done by hand (see below) or on a sewing machine using a zigzag stitch. Frayed threads at the edge of the work can get tangled up with embroidery thread on the back and are a nuisance. Before you start to stitch, iron the fabric to remove any stubborn creases.

3 Find the centre of the fabric, as this is where the first stitch will be worked. Stitching the central stitch of a design in the centre of the fabric ensures that there will be an even amount of spare fabric all round the design, which is important at the mounting stage. Fold the fabric into four and mark the central point temporarily with a pin.

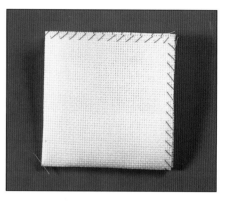

4 Using light-coloured tacking (basting) thread, mark the vertical and horizontal lines that meet in the centre of the fabric. Remove the pin. Once all the cross stitching is complete, the tacking threads should be removed.

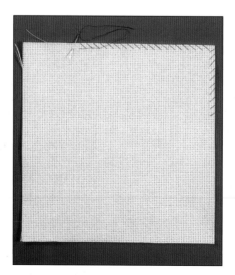

Threads

All the designs in this book were sewn using stranded cotton. DMC, Anchor and Madeira stranded cottons are readily available. These are six-stranded mercerized cottons with a lustrous finish, which can be separated into single strands or groups of two or more strands. They are colourfast and are usually sold in 8m skeins. Dye lots vary, so ensure you buy enough of each colour to finish your design.

Gold and silver threads are useful when embroidering details such as buttons, jewellery, buckles and so on. There are many manufacturers producing metallic threads, including DMC, Anchor, Madeira and Kreinik. Interesting effects can be achieved by combining stranded cotton with blending filaments, creating a subtle gleam and sparkle.

Choosing Thread Colours

Choice of colour is a very personal affair and there are no hard and fast rules. It might help to consider the room where the embroidery is to hang, and build a colour scheme to harmonize with existing decoration and furnishings. Several shades of the same colour can sometimes be more effective than a completely random selection. If you doubt your own judgement look for a design whose colours you like in a book that gives a colour key. Make a note of the colour numbers for future reference; you will then know that these colours are pleasing to you and work well together. Colour keys have been included for the charted designs in the main chapters of this book but only general colour guidance is given for the charted designs in the Motif Library.

Q: How many strands of thread do I use?

Your cross stitches must cover the fabric sufficiently, but not be so thick that they enlarge the holes in the fabric. Remember that four cross stitches and a number of backstitches may all occupy the same hole. The following table gives guidance on how many strands of stranded cotton to use with various fabric counts. Work a few sample stitches in the corner of your fabric to check coverage.

Fabric	Number of strands of stranded cotton
11-count Aida or 22-count Hardanger (over two Hardanger threads)	3 strands for cross stitch and 2 for backstitch
14-count Aida or 28-count linen (over two linen threads)	2 or 3 strands for cross stitch and 1 for backstitch
16-count Aida or 32-count linen (over two linen threads)	2 strands for cross stitch and 1 for backstitch
18-count Aida or 36-count linen (over two linen threads)	1 or 2 strands for cross stitch and 1 for backstitch

BUYING THREADS

There are so many wonderful threads available today, in a huge range of colours and types, all just waiting for you to try them. Many smaller companies produce interesting speciality threads.

- When you buy your threads find a well-stocked shop with a large range of colours and choose colours in full daylight. Hold them together in your hand to see if they harmonize with each other. Colours held in the hand can look brighter in the skein than when they are worked in small quantities alongside other colours.

- Lay the skeins on the fabric that will be the background, as this will, in turn, have an effect on the colours when they are embroidered on to it.

- Many people choose to imitate the pastel shades of old samplers, not realising that these colours are the result of years of fading; originally they would have been quite bright. So if you are sewing for posterity, avoid using very pale shades.

- If you are sewing on an off-white or cream-coloured fabric, very pale colours are hard to distinguish from the background. For this reason you may have to choose deeper shades than your original choice, but the colours can still be soft as there are many deeper shades that are neither harsh nor garish.

- To avoid losing spare strands after you have cut a length from the skein and have separated the strands, make a thread holder. Old greetings cards with holes punched down the sides will do the job. Write the yarn shade number beside each occupied hole for future reference.

Other Equipment

Cross stitch embroidery requires very little equipment, which makes it easy to do almost anywhere. The basics you'll need are described here.

Needles

You will need a blunt tapestry needle that will slip easily through the holes in your fabric without piercing or splitting the threads. The needle should be sufficiently fine to slip through the holes without enlarging or distorting them. Finer needles have a higher number on the packet (26); thicker needles have lower numbers (18). Buy several; they get lost and have been known to break.

Scissors

You will need dressmaking scissors if you are going to cut your fabric to size before sewing, and a pair of sharp, fine-pointed embroidery scissors. The latter will be used for cutting thread from the skein and when finishing off a thread in the embroidery. If they are not sharp they will 'chew' the thread. Messy finishing on the back of the work is to be avoided as it can show through on the right side when the work is mounted. Embroidery scissors are also used for, horror of horrors, unpicking. The points must be fine enough to slip under the offending stitch to cut it. Never be tempted to use a stitch ripper as this will distort your existing stitching and your fabric.

tip

When sewing, if you hang your embroidery scissors around your neck on a ribbon, this will save hunting for them every time they are put down.

Embroidery Hoops

The use of an embroidery hoop ensures that you produce accurate and even stitching and that the minimum amount of pressing will be necessary when the work is completed. Some people, however, prefer the freedom of working without a hoop or frame. Use a hoop only if the whole area to be stitched fits easily inside it: if the hoop has to be moved over existing embroidery the stitches risk being flattened and distorted by the pressure of the hoop, so for larger embroideries use a frame. (See page 96 for decorating a hoop and using it as a frame.)

1 To use a hoop, first, bind the inner hoop with a white bias cotton tape to protect the fabric and prevent slipping.

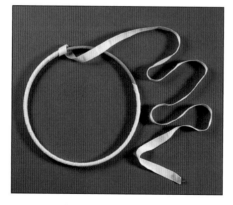

2 Lay fabric over the inner hoop ring, positioning it so that the centre of the fabric lies in the centre of the hoop.

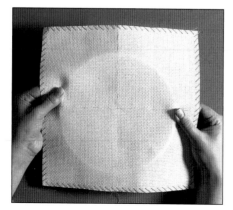

3 Place the outer ring of the hoop over the inner ring, with the tension screw at the top. Press the outer hoop down over the inner and tighten the screw, adjusting the fabric so that it is taut as a drum. Check that the horizontal and vertical threads have not been distorted in the process. Reposition the fabric if they have.

Flexi-hoops

Flexi-hoops are circular, oval, or square plastic hoops that consist of a rigid inner hoop and a flexible outer hoop. They come in a variety of sizes, colours and finishes and are often used instead of wooden embroidery hoops for working very small cross stitch projects.

To use a flexi-hoop, place the fabric over the inner hoop and ease the outer hoop on to the inner hoop to hold work tautly in place.

tip

When stitching is finished, a flexi-hoop can be used as a decorative frame for the work.

Embroidery Frames

Rectangular frames come in many sizes; some of the larger ones have a floor stand, allowing you to hold one hand at the front of the work and one at the back, which speeds up the stabbing motion. They consist of two wooden stretchers at the sides and two wooden rollers held in place by wing-nuts or pegs. The rollers each have a piece of webbing nailed to them. If the fabric is wider than the webbing, you will need a larger frame. The fabric can be any length as the excess is wound on to the rollers when it is not being worked.

1 To use a frame, first, hem your fabric to strengthen the edges so that it will not pull apart when it is laced to the frame.

2 Sew the top of the fabric to the top piece of the frame's webbing, and do the same at the bottom, matching the centre of the fabric to the centre of the webbing. Do not be tempted to use drawing pins or staples to attach the fabric – threads may be pulled and ruin the fabric.

3 Lace the sides of the fabric to the frame stretchers with strong thread such as buttonhole or linen thread, and when both sides are laced, tighten the threads and the wing-nuts so that the fabric is stretched taut. Tie the ends of the threads firmly to the stretchers. When working a long design it may be necessary to roll completed stitching on to one of the rollers to expose more fabric for work. In this case a sheet of white tissue paper rolled into the back of the work will prevent crushing the stitches.

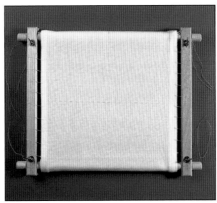

tip

If working without a hoop or frame, stitch with a continuous stitching motion and an even tension. Take care not to pull the thread so tight that the fabric holes are enlarged and distorted, nor to work so slackly that the stitches are loose.

LIGHTING

Trying to embroider in the gloom results in tired eyes, often followed by the discouragement of having to unpick mistakes. The following advice should help.

- Sit near a window to work during daylight hours.

- Those who are tempted to sew outdoors on a fine day are in peril of staining their work; beware of perspiring fingers, children lurching around with ice creams and fizzy drinks and the less obvious danger of a bird with an upset stomach flying overhead!

- When sewing at night, work under a good lamp, positioned on your left if you are right-handed, and on your right if you are left-handed, so that you are not working in your own shadow. Daylight bulbs, which simulate the clear, bright light of day time, are useful if you routinely stitch in the evenings.

- Use a magnifier if necessary, especially if you are working on a fine fabric, such as a 36-count linen. Magnifiers are available on stands, as table-top items or can hang around your neck; some models have a built-in light.

- If you are still struggling to see the work clearly, give in gracefully and go and have your eyes tested.

Preparing to Sew **29**

Sewing the Design

The main stitch used in the sewing of your design will be full cross stitch.
You will also need to know how to form a three-quarter cross stitch, how
to backstitch and how to make French knots. Practise any stitches that
are unfamiliar to you before you begin to sew your own design.

Starting and Finishing

Starting and finishing work neatly without bulging knots is important
to avoid unsightly lumps showing on the finished piece.

Knotless Loop Start

This method of starting to stitch is very
neat and easy and is used if you are
working with an even number of strands
of thread.

Cut the stranded cotton roughly twice
the length you would normally need and
separate one strand. Double the strand
and thread your needle with the two ends.
Now pierce your fabric from the wrong side
where you intend to place your first stitch,
leaving the looped end at the back of the
work. Return your needle to the wrong side
after forming a half cross stitch and pass
the needle through the waiting loop (Fig 1).

Away Waste Knot Start

This technique is used when starting a
new thread in bare fabric, where there are
no existing stitches on to which the new
thread can be anchored. It can be used
with any number of strands of thread.

Insert the needle, leaving a short tail
or knot on the front of the work. Bring the
needle out where you wish the stitching
to start. Now stitch in the direction of the
knot, catching the thread at the back as
you sew (Fig 2). After a few stitches the
thread will be secure and the loose end
or knot can be trimmed off neatly on the
back of the work.

Changing Colour or Thread

Where a new colour butts up against
existing stitches, the new thread can be
run through the back of two or three of
the stitches already worked. Make a small
backstitch to secure it and bring the new
thread to the right side to start work.

Finishing Stitching

To finish stitching without using a knot,
run the thread through the backs of three
or four stitches that have just been worked,
taking care not to distort them (Fig 3). Take
a small backstitch to secure the end, and
then cut off the thread close to the fabric.

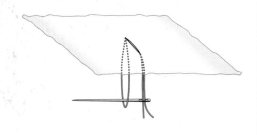

Fig 1 Knotless loop start

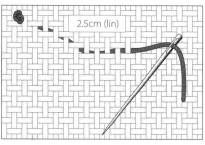

Fig 2 Away waste knot start

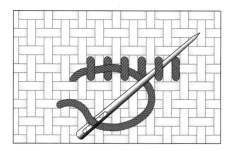

Fig 3 Finishing off a thread neatly

Cross Stitch

One completely filled square on your chart indicates one full cross stitch on your fabric. When working on evenweave linen or cotton, work the full cross stitch over two threads (Fig 4), on Aida over one block of threads (Fig 5) and on Hardanger fabric over two pairs of threads (Fig 6).

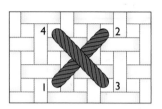

Fig 4 A full cross stitch worked on evenweave linen

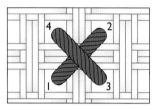

Fig 5 A full cross stitch worked on Aida fabric

Fig 6 A full cross stitch worked on Hardanger fabric

tip

The first few stitches are sometimes confusing when working on evenweave but you will soon get used to seeing threads in pairs and mistakes will become obvious.

Cross stitch can be worked in rows rather than individually. When working rows of full cross stitches, bring the needle out at the left-hand side of the row of stitches to be worked. On evenweave, insert the needle two threads up and two threads across. Pull the thread through to the back. Bring the needle out two threads down. A half cross has been formed and you are ready to work the next stitch in the line. Continue working half crosses until the end of the line is reached, then return to form the complete crosses, working from right to left and using the same holes as before (Fig 7). All stitches interlock or 'hold hands', sharing holes with their neighbours, unless they are single stitches worked on their own.

Fig 7 Working a line of full cross stitches in two journeys on evenweave

This colourful detail from The Things I Sow (page 44) shows the basic stitches described in this section – beautifully worked cross stitch, backstitch and French knots.

Spaces on the chart indicate unworked ground, i.e., bare fabric, so for each space leave two threads of evenweave (or one block if working on Aida) uncovered (Fig 8).

Fig 8 Spaces on the chart indicate bare fabric

With cross stitch it is important that the bottom stitch slants in the same direction throughout the work; if your bottom stitches all slant from left to right, your top stitches will automatically all slant from right to left, giving your work a regular appearance and a pleasing sheen. It doesn't matter which direction you choose as long as you are consistent. Take care if you turn your work sideways, when embroidering a border for instance, that you maintain the correct direction.

tip

A large full cross stitch worked as a sample in the turning allowance will show you at a glance which way your bottom stitch should be lying.

Three-Quarter Cross Stitch

This stitch is indicated on your chart by a right-angled triangle. The first half of the cross stitch is formed in the usual way, but the second 'quarter' stitch is brought across and down into the central hole (Fig 9). The rule of having the bottom stitches always slanting in the same direction is thus sometimes broken, but by bringing the 'quarter' stitch over the top, the longer bottom stitch is anchored down firmly giving a neater effect. Where the chart indicates two three-quarter stitches together, these are worked sharing the same central hole and occupying the space of one whole cross stitch. Fig 10 shows a charted combination of full cross stitch and three-quarter cross stitch.

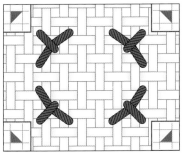

Fig 9 Examples of three-quarter cross stitches on evenweave

Fig 10 A combination of full cross stitch and three-quarter cross stitch

Backstitch

The use of backstitch is indicated on your chart by a solid line. When all the full and three-quarter cross stitches have been worked in one area of the design, backstitch can be worked around or over them to add detail and definition. Backstitch is worked either over two threads or one, depending on the direction indicated on the chart. It can be worked vertically, horizontally or diagonally.

Bring the needle out at 1 and in at 2. Bring it out again at 3 and in at 4 (Fig 11). Continue this sequence in the direction indicated by your chart.

Backstitch can also be used to work lettering (Fig 12), either over two threads of evenweave (one block of Aida) or over just one thread, which enables you to stitch longer poems or verses.

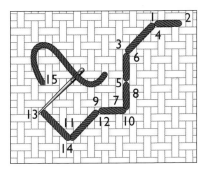

Fig 11 Working backstitch on evenweave

Fig 12 Using backstitch for lettering

A white tennis ball, when sewn on to a light-coloured fabric, requires both outlining for definition and detailing to distinguish it from a golf ball (Fig 13). For added versatility, backstitch can be worked over two threads in one direction and one thread in another.

Fig 13 Backstitch used for definition and detail

Sometimes the unused holes within the cross stitches are used, for example when sewing mouths on to faces, the stitch in this case being sewn over one thread (Fig 14). A single backstitch can be used on its own for details such as animal whiskers and ships' rigging. Always use fewer strands of threads for backstitch than you have used for the cross stitches.

Fig 14 Using backstitch and French knots to stitch a face

French Knots

The use of this stitch will be indicated on your chart by a circle or knot shape, usually coloured. Work French knots with one strand of thread. For larger knots try using two strands or try a thicker needle. Too many twists around the needle will not produce a satisfactory round knot, so experiment beforehand to get the effect you want.

To sew a French knot, bring the needle out one thread to the right of where you want the knot to lie (Fig 15). Depending on the size of the knot you require, slip the needle once or twice under the thread so that the twists lie snugly around the needle. Without allowing the thread to untwist, insert the needle back into the fabric one thread to the left of where you started (or part of an Aida block) and pull the thread through to the back. If you do not work the knot with one thread to support it, you risk the knot sinking into the hole and getting lost on the back of the work.

Starting to Sew Your Design

Your first stitch will normally be the central stitch on your chart and will be sewn in the centre of your fabric, which you have already marked with tacking (basting) threads. If the central square on your chart happens to be a blank space, you will have to count from the centre to the nearest area to be stitched and begin there. To count accurately across areas of bare fabric it is easiest to thread your needle with tacking thread and, counting carefully, work the correct number of dummy crosses to the point where you wish to start. With the correct position found you can later remove the tacking-thread crosses, leaving only the intended spaces.

When the first piece of your design is correctly positioned on your fabric, you are free to proceed in any direction you choose. Some people like to work the border first; others leave it to the end. When sewing the border, check your work

frequently as you progress, for it is very disheartening to find you have miscounted and the border will not join up.

Beginners may find it helpful to work a test piece, as shown in Fig 16. The figure includes the use of full cross stitch and three-quarter cross stitch, with backstitch and French knots for details, thus covering the main techniques. So that your work can be put to good use, alter the colours to suit someone you know, and you will have the beginnings of a greetings card for her. When you are satisfied that your embroidered figure compares favourably with the example shown here, you will be able to tackle with confidence any design in this book.

tip
It is important to work from the centre of a chart and the centre of the fabric to ensure that the whole design will fit on the fabric.

Fig 15 Working a French knot

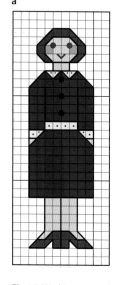

a

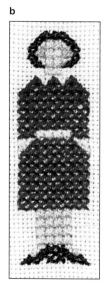

b

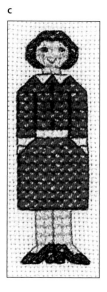

c

Fig 16 Working a test piece:
a) work from the chart;
b) sew all the full cross stitches and three-quarter cross stitches;
c) now add backstitch and French knots to complete your figure

TOP TIPS FOR PERFECT PICTURES

DO ✓

- **Do** wash your hands before each work session.

- **Do** press stubborn creases out of your fabric before you work your first stitch. Then, when the work is complete it will only need a light pressing to avoid flattening the stitches.

- **Do** finish off neatly after each separate area has been worked. Thread can be brought from one area to another across the back of the work, without finishing off, only if there is an existing line of stitching behind which the thread can be hidden. Take care not to distort existing stitches as you bring your thread through the back of these stitches.

- **Do** cut off threads close to the fabric with sharp embroidery scissors and cut off loose ends at once, before they get caught up in other work.

- **Do** use sharp embroidery scissors and tweezers to remove any mistakes.

- **Do** allow the needle to dangle upside down from the fabric occasionally to remove any twists on the thread. Threads cover better when lying flat, whereas a twisted thread will produce uneven stitches.

- **Do** roll your embroidery in acid-free tissue when it is not being worked and protect it from accidents. If it is on a hoop or frame, cover it between sessions to keep it clean.

- **Do** leave until last all areas to be stitched in white thread, to keep them clean and sparkling.

- **Do** relax and enjoy your work!

DON'T ✗

- **Don't** leave your needle in the fabric when you put it away. It could leave a mark or rust if left for any length of time, unless you are using a gold-plated needle.

- **Don't** use more than 30cm (12in) of thread in your needle. It will twist and tangle and the end near the needle will be worn and frayed before you use it.

- **Don't** work the background. In cross stitch embroidery the background is left bare.

- **Don't** jump your thread across the back of bare fabric from one area to another. When the work is mounted, a trail will be visible through the fabric and will spoil its appearance.

- **Don't** pull the fabric threads together, tugging too hard on the needle as you sew; lacy holes belong in pulled-thread work, not in cross stitch embroidery.

- **Don't** sew with unpicked thread. It will be worn and kinked and won't produce neat stitches.

- **Don't** use a stitch ripper to remove mistakes – you will distort your fabric and existing stitches.

- **Don't** fold your work for storage. Stubborn creases will develop that will be difficult to remove and will eventually weaken the fabric.

- **Don't** forget to remove any tacking (basting) threads when all stitching is complete.

- **Don't** be surprised if you become completely addicted to this work!

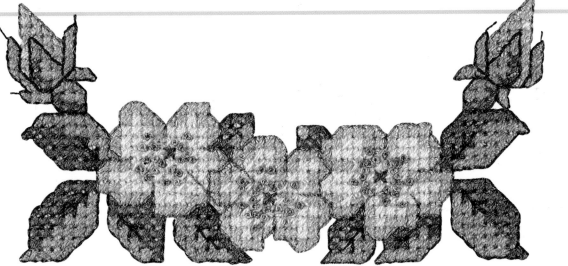

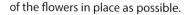

Decorated Initials

Being small, initials are quick and satisfying to stitch and will give you the confidence to continue with something more ambitious. The designs in this chapter offer three alphabets from which to choose an initial, and examples of how these can be used to produce a charming, personalized result.

Bold Alphabet

This alphabet (charted on page 43) has been designed to be accompanied by a motif of your choice, the only decoration on it being small flowers, which are easily omitted if you want to leave the letter plain. These letters can be used singly, as decorated initials, or can be put together into names or messages. There is also a nursery alphabet on page 139 which can be used in a similar way.

Decorative Ideas

The alphabet is charted in strong colours but these can be changed in a trice.

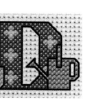

- For a gardening friend, position a trowel and watering with their initial, leaving as many of the flowers in place as possible.

- For a cat lover, sit a cat in front of an upright section of any initial. Add a kitten too if you wish.

- For a railway enthusiast or a child mad about trains, position a train on an initial. The flowers can be removed to allow the addition of some steam and a signal.

- For a child, place some toys with any initial or lean a baby against an initial and fill any gaps with bricks. Some toys are charted on page 130.

- For someone who has a floral name such as Violet, Rose or Daisy, place the relevant flower on an initial and add a few leaves.

- For a musician or violinist, place a violin over the upright of any initial and scatter a few musical notes around the letter.

- For a cricketer or other sportsman, use the uprights of any initial as a background for a cricket bat, ball and stumps or other relevant equipment.

- For a birthday treat, add a cake with candles and a present to an initial. The S has no single upright section so symbols can be placed on either side of the centre section, as shown here.

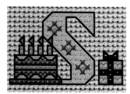

DECORATING AN INITIAL

Follow these guidelines when decorating a letter and look on page 42 and also through the Motif Library for ideas on motifs to use.

1 First choose your initial and draw it out on to graph paper.

2 Next choose the decorative motif you want to use with the initial. You could invent your own or find something suitable in this book.

3 Draw out your motif on to graph paper and cut it out. Move the motif over the initial until you find a good position for it. You will notice that most of the letters have at least one thick upright section and this is generally a good

position. Where there is more than one upright you could use more than one motif.

4 If you wish to use one of the motifs shown, but it appears on an initial that's not what you want, draw out your initial and add the motif to the new initial.

5 When you are happy with the position of the motif, stick it into place over the initial. Tidy up the drawing and colour it in. Your pattern is now ready to sew.

Floral Alphabet

This alphabet (charted opposite), shows how you can experiment with initials, adding different flowers and butterflies to the letter of your choice; the flowers are interchangeable, as are the butterflies. Colour codes have been given in the key but do experiment with your own colour choices. The letters are perfect for spelling out names. Many names have the same letter used more than once, so rather than sew the same pattern twice, and to give variety, change the repeated letter by taking a flower from another letter and substituting it for the one you've already used. Use the butterflies to fill any spaces created by the positioning of the letters. A lower case alphabet has been charted on page 142, which would be suitable to use with all three large alphabets to create your own messages. There are other alphabets on pages 67 and 140.

Decorative Ideas

The Floral Alphabet uses a limited colour range, so would be perfect to experiment with different colours, threads and fabrics.

- Decorate a box or trinket pot lid. There are many such items available with inserts for embroidery – look in your local craft shop, in stitching magazines and on-line.

- Use evenweave and Aida bands to decorate towels or other household linen with decorative alphabets, forming words, such as 'Welcome' for a guest towel. Bands are available with different types of edgings and in various colours and only have to be turned under at each end and sewn on to the towel.

- A framed initial (see above) is simple to do and there are many frames available that add the perfect finishing touch to a small piece of embroidery. Take care that your design will fit your chosen frame – see page 20.

- Napkin rings (below) are perfect for special family occasions or favourite guests. Stitch a decorated initial on a strip of evenweave or Aida (or on a band) and make up into a napkin ring (see page 98).

tip
Take care that whatever motif you choose to put with your initial that it does not obliterate the initial and make it unrecognisable.

tip
When you sew a design on to an evenweave or Aida band, find the centre of the band and the centre of the letter and work outwards from there.

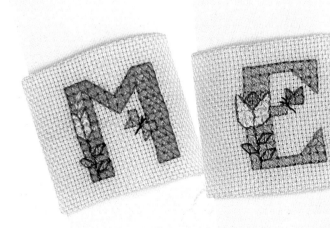

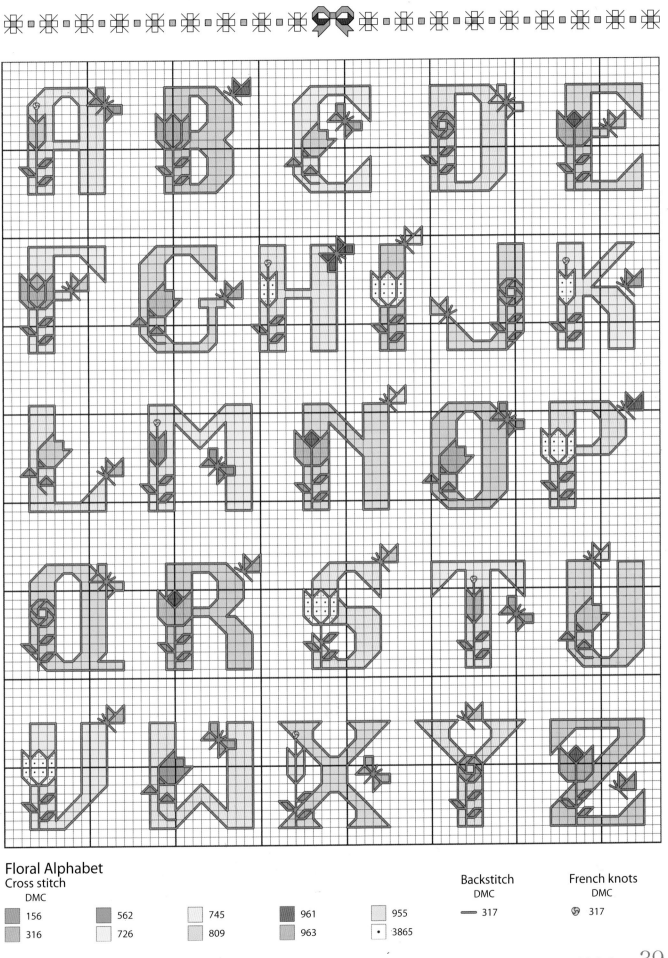

Floral Alphabet
Cross stitch

DMC					Backstitch	French knots
					DMC	DMC
▨ 156	▨ 562	▨ 745	▨ 961	▨ 955	— 317	✬ 317
▨ 316	▨ 726	▨ 809	▨ 963	• 3865		

Seasonal Alphabet

This alphabet (charted opposite) can be decorated in a similar way to the Bold Alphabet but is also ideal for a variety of seasonal motifs, so you can use the alphabet for gifts and cards all year round. The colour of the letters can be changed to suit the season – perhaps a fresh lemon yellow for spring, an azure blue for summer, a rich russet for autumn and a festive green for winter.

tip

Decorating an initial is a good way to experiment with different types of threads, such as shiny rayons, glittering metallics or subtle variegated threads – perfect for festive occasions.

Decorative Ideas

Various seasonal motifs are provided overleaf for you to use with the Seasonal Alphabet but look through the Motif Library for other ideas. No key is given for the motifs as you will want to choose your own colour schemes.

- Surround an initial or name with flowers, as shown below, either by creating your own floral design following the advice on pages 22–23 or using one of the bands on pages 134–137. Draw the border out on to separate long strips of graph paper and position them around the name. Add a few extra flowers to soften the corners. If you are stitching a short name you can make the border smaller – simply

use fewer pattern repeats at the top and the bottom. Conversely, for a longer name, add more pattern repeats.

- Stitch all the letters of the seasonal alphabet and choose suitable motifs (from overleaf or the Motif Library) to create a stunning seasonal sampler. As a finishing touch, surround the whole design with a double-line border.

- Create gifts and cards for Easter, Christmas or other seasonal occasions by placing suitable motifs with the letters. The Christmas card here shows how easy this is. The lower case alphabet on page 142 could be used to create a longer message.

tip

An easy way to bring colour to a design is to stitch a simple double-line border with variegated threads, and see the colours change from stitch to stitch.

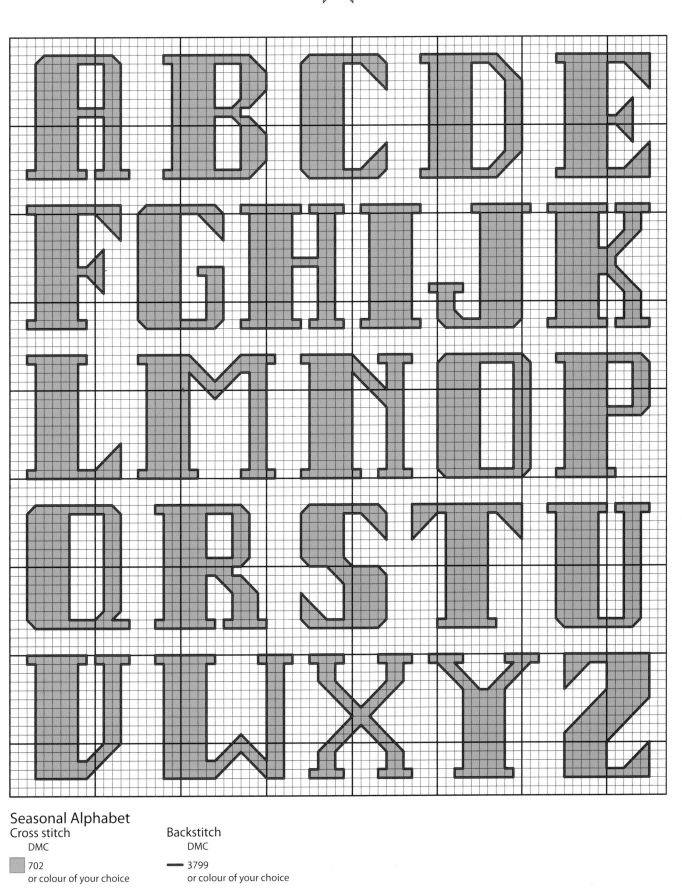

Seasonal Alphabet

Cross stitch
DMC

702
or colour of your choice

Backstitch
DMC

— 3799
or colour of your choice

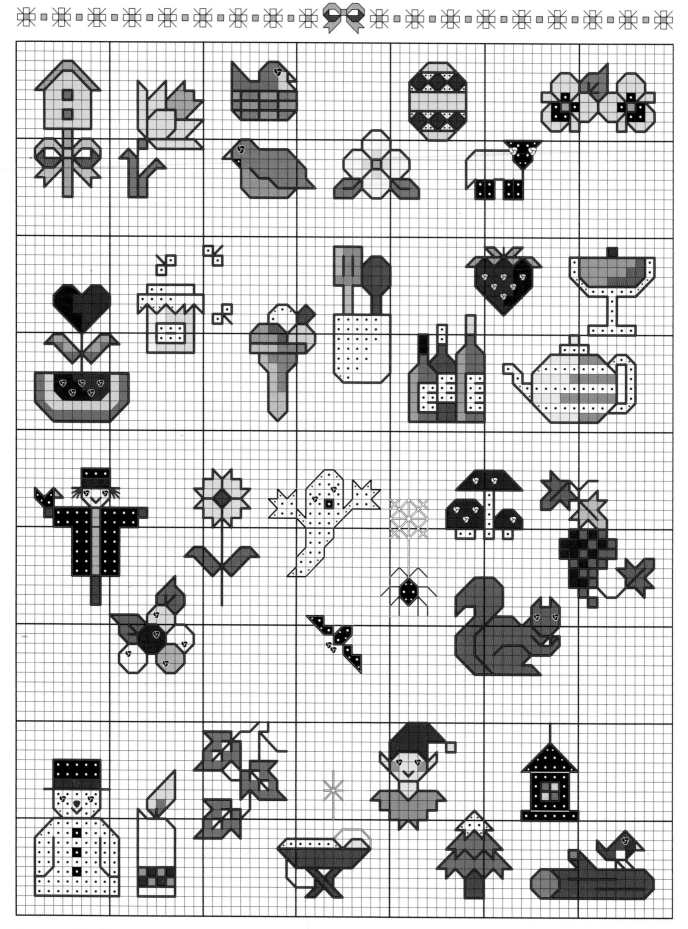

Seasonal Motifs   Use the colours suggested here or select your own shades

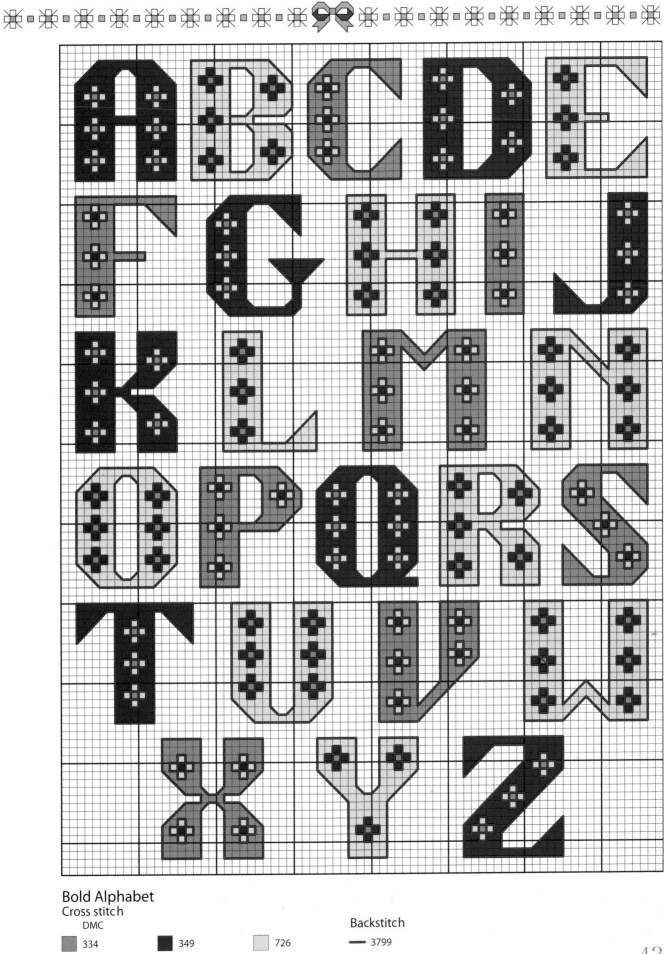

Bold Alphabet
Cross stitch

DMC

■ 334   ■ 349   □ 726

Backstitch

— 3799

Using Texts

Many of us have a favourite text that we would like to embroider but the chances are that it won't be available ready charted. This chapter shows you how to produce a design for a text of your own. The treatment of three texts is explained so you will be able to follow the process and chart your own text (see page 46 for the process in a nutshell).

The Things I Sow

The Things I Sow

Stitch count	75h x 108w
Design size	14 x 19.5cm
	(5½ x 7¾in)
Fabric	28-count cream or
	off-white evenweave
	(or a 14-count Aida)

Work over two fabric threads (or one block of Aida), using two strands of stranded cotton for full and three-quarter cross stitches following the chart on pages 50–51. Work French knots and backstitches with one strand.

tip
When backstitching a text don't be tempted to carry the thread from word to word across the back of the fabric as it will show from the front. Finish off each word neatly.

The Things I Sow

This amusing verse might strike a chord with gardeners and appeared in a gardening magazine, authorship unknown.

Each of the three designs in this chapter has a different border, designed to cater for a variety of tastes, and each can be filled with wording other than that suggested here.

The Things I Sow has quite a long verse, so a backstitch alphabet was chosen for lettering. The lettering was drawn out and positioned on the master sheet, as described on page 20. A border of wild flowers was assembled around the lettering, the plants traced from botanical books on to graphed tracing paper, squared up and cut out separately. They were placed on the master sheet, shuffled around and overlapped to get a rectangular shape

The things I sow
Somehow don't grow,
I'm sorely disenchanted –
But, oh, what luck
I have with stuff
I never even planted.

that fitted with the lettering. Some fauna crept in to fill the odd awkward gap.

This border is in complete contrast to the rosebud border shown on page 47, but still allows you to substitute your own text as the border can be expanded to fit longer texts. To expand this wildflower border horizontally, when you have copied it out on to graph paper, make a cut to the left of the daisy and ferns at the bottom. Cut between the butterfly and ivy at the top, to separate the left-hand side of the border from the right. Insert extra graph paper to get the size you require, and fill the gaps with an extra leaf or two. To expand the border vertically, give all the plants longer stalks, but take care not to distort the balance of the composition.

The things I sow
Somehow don't grow
I'm sorely disenchanted—
But, oh, what luck
I have with stuff
I never even planted.

Gather Ye Rosebuds

Many old cross stitch texts of the 'Thou Shalt Not' variety, are of a stern, forbidding nature and high moral tone. Preferring a positive exhortation to a negative one, the following lines by Robert Herrick have long been favourites of mine.

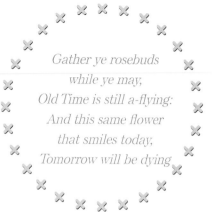

Gather ye rosebuds
while ye may,
Old Time is still a-flying:
And this same flower
that smiles today,
Tomorrow will be dying

Gather Ye Rosebuds

Stitch count	97h x 146w
Design size	17.5 x 26.5cm
	(7 x 10½in)
Fabric	28-count cream or
	off-white evenweave
	(or a 14-count Aida)

Work over two fabric threads (or one block of Aida), using two strands of stranded cotton for full and three-quarter cross stitches following the chart on page 52. Work French knots and backstitches with one strand.

The rosebuds were drawn out to form a regular trellis pattern with an inner line representing a threaded ribbon tied in a bow at the top in the centre. The border could be filled with any text that fits, or could be expanded to take a longer text.

The design needed some decorative 'fillers'. Rosebuds already appeared in the border, so roses in full bloom were used to fill the gaps at the end of lines 2 and 3. Dead roses are not very inspiring, but they are followed by rose-hips, which are decorative, so these were chosen to fill the last two gaps. The life cycle of the rose is thus pictorially represented to echo the sense of the lines.

tip

The backstitch alphabet used for The Things I Sow and Gather Ye Rosebuds is charted on page 67 but there are many other alphabets in the book that you could use for your own texts.

DESIGNING A CHART OF A TEXT

These instructions can be applied to all three texts in this chapter or words of your own choosing. See pages 22–23 if you need a reminder on designing a chart.

1 When starting to design a chart of a text, decide whether to use a cross stitch or a backstitch alphabet for the lettering. Because all three of the verses in this chapter are quite long, a backstitch alphabet was used. If a cross stitch alphabet had been used, the design would have been too large to fit the space where the finished embroidery was to hang.

2 Draw out your lettering, putting each line on a separate strip of graph paper, ready to cut to size later.

3 Choose a border. The subject matter of a text can often suggest a suitable border. In the case of 'Gather Ye Rosebuds', rosebuds were the obvious choice.

4 With the text chosen, fit the lettering inside the border. If a line is too long and has to be split, take some heed of the sense and split it at an appropriate point.

5 When you have positioned your lettering inside the border, check that you are happy with the spacing between letters, between words, and between lines. If you need larger spaces there is no need to erase your work and re-draw it; simply cut your strip of lettering at the appropriate point and paste in some extra graph paper to enlarge the space. If spaces are too generous, again cut the strip at the appropriate point and overlap the cut edges to narrow the gap. Check that your lettering is not too close to the border at any point.

6 When the lettering is in position there may be spaces that would look better filled with a decorative symbol. When deciding how to fill any gaps, go back to the sense of the lines to choose something appropriate – some useful fillers are charted on page 138.

7 Lastly, give credit where it is due and include the name of the author of your text in your design.

God Gave Us Memory

This text was planned in the same way as the other two examples, taking account of the space needed for the lettering and using a motif that suited the quotation (see the steps on page 46 to remind you of the process). The cross stitch design is quite small but the highly decorative mount enhances the design and fits the theme beautifully. If you wish to use the same alphabet but change the verse, the letters are charted on page 67.

*God gave us
Memory
that we might have
Roses in
December*

God Gave Us Memory

Stitch count 67h x 50w
Design size 12 x 9cm
(4¾ x 3½in)
Fabric 28-count cream or
off-white evenweave
(or a 14-count Aida)

Work over two fabric threads (or one block of Aida), using two strands of stranded cotton for full and three-quarter cross stitches following the chart on page 53. Work French knots and backstitches with one strand.

tip

If you are working on an evenweave linen remember that you can stitch lettering over just one thread, which will result in smaller lettering but will allow you to use longer texts.

OTHER TEXTS TO TRY

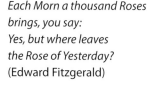

There are thousands of texts to choose from – your local library is a good source and of course the Internet will give you access to an overwhelming choice. The Motif Library contains many ideas for decorating texts and verses.

*All things bright and beautiful,
All things great and small,
All things wise and wonderful,
The Lord God made them all.*
(C.F. Alexander)

*How doth the little busy bee
Improve each shining hour,
And gather honey all day
From every opening flower!*
(Isaac Watts)

*The kiss of the sun for pardon,
The song of the birds for mirth,
One is nearer God's Heart in a garden
Than anywhere else on earth.*
(Dorothy Gurney)

*To see a World in a grain of sand,
And a Heaven in a wild flower,
Hold Infinity in the palm
of your hand,
And Eternity in an hour.*
(William Blake)

*And I wove the thing
to random rhyme,
For the Rose is Beauty,
the Gardener, Time.*
(Austin Dobson)

*Each Morn a thousand Roses
brings, you say:
Yes, but where leaves
the Rose of Yesterday?*
(Edward Fitzgerald)

*And I will make thee beds of roses
And a thousand fragrant posies.*
(Christopher Marlowe)

*One thing is certain, that Life flies;
One thing is certain,
and the Rest is Lies;
The Flower that once has blown
for ever dies.*
(Edward Fitzgerald)

*Full many a flower is born
to blush unseen,
And waste its sweetness
on the desert air.*
(Thomas Gray)

*Flowers of all hue,
and without thorn the rose.*
(John Milton)

*God Almighty first planted a garden;
and, indeed, it is the purest
of human pleasures.*
(Francis Bacon)

The Things I Sow
Cross stitch

DMC

· blanc	415	X 472	⊡ 553	⊓ 666	742	O 890	⟋ 989
● 310	433	⊖ 550	554	△ 727	746	898	3326
321	470	552	561	738	800	N 971	3787

Backstitch

DMC

⟋ blanc	— 470	— 776	— 3787
— 310	— 550	— 890	
— 433	— 666	— 971	

French knots

DMC

🌀 310	🌀 890
🌀 433	🌀 3787
🌀 746	

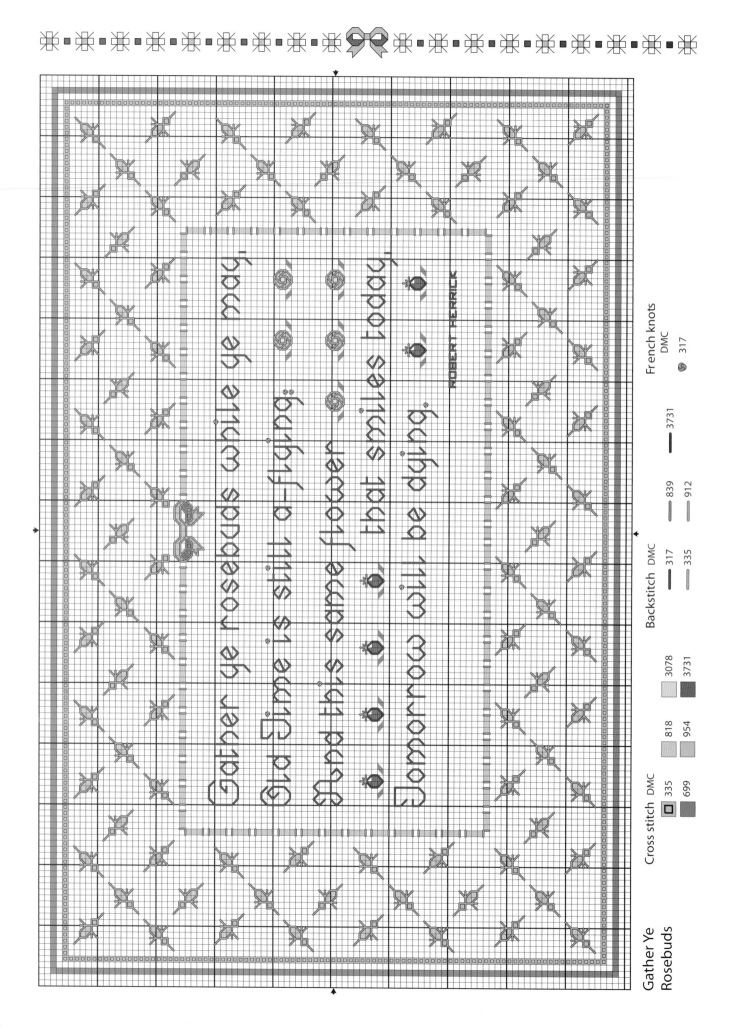

Gather ye rosebuds while ye may,
Old Time is still a-flying;
And this same flower that smiles today
Tomorrow will be dying.

ROBERT HERRICK

Gather Ye Rosebuds

Cross stitch DMC
☐ 335
■ 699
▨ 3078
▨ 3731
▨ 818
▨ 954

Backstitch DMC
—— 317
—— 335
—— 839
—— 912

French knots DMC
๑ 317

God Gave Us Memory

Cross stitch

DMC

- • 948
- ◇ 3051
- ▨ 3364
- ▨ 3713

Backstitch

DMC

- — 935
- — 3688

French knots

DMC

- ⊚ 729

House and Family

During the 18th and 19th centuries many samplers were worked by young people as classroom exercises to teach needlework. A large number survive today in museums and private collections, or as heirlooms passed down through families. This chapter shows you how to create your own heirloom sampler as a record of *your* house and family.

Old Samplers

Samplers from past centuries are all highly valued and of interest both to needleworkers and those who study social history, giving a glimpse into life as it was lived in those days.

A typical sampler design consisted of a floral border, inside which were stitched an alphabet and numbers, reflecting classroom life. Often a house was represented, which may have been the home of the embroiderer or a local landmark. Animals, flowers and other traditional symbols, each with a meaning, were often included, together with a motto or verse of high moral tone.

This watercolour of my childhood home, painted by Helen Lodge in 1961, was used as the basis for my childhood home sampler, shown opposite.

Your House and Family Sampler

Embroidering a house and family sampler today gives an opportunity to make a statement about your family, your home and the life led in it, in a contemporary style that will be of interest to future generations.

Many kits and patterns are available for you to sew but they are generally based on older sampler designs that have been worked many times before and so have nothing new to say. The time involved in sewing a kit and in sewing your own design will be the same, but the satisfaction of producing a unique piece of work for posterity will be far greater than just producing a copy of someone else's work.

To make a truly personal and up-to-date statement you will have to undertake the design work yourself, and this chapter gives detailed stepped instructions. Follow the process used to produce the design for the sampler of my childhood home and then adapt them to your circumstances.

For those of you new to cross stitch and designing your own work there is a design on page 61 (charted on page 66) for you to stitch first. The simplistic house is mostly backstitch and you can try your hand at changing the figures within the house by referring to the advice on page 58.

Designing a House and Family Sampler – in a nutshell...

The following four pages give detailed advice about designing your own house and family sampler. Before starting, make sure you have read the general design instructions in Designing the Charts pages 14–23.

Step 1

Make a list of ingredients, i.e., a list of everything you would like to record in your design under the headings given below. Your list needs to be flexible as some items may not fit, or may not be suitable for some other reason, in which case it is better to save discarded material for another occasion rather than try to cram everything in willy-nilly.

- **House** – your present or a previous home
- **Family** – immediate or extended family
- **Pets** – the more the merrier
- **Garden** – assorted flora and fauna
- **Location** – town, county or area where the house is situated
- **Nationalities** – countries of origin of family members, or which have influenced family life
- **Work** – the occupations of the various family members
- **Interests** – hobbies and pastimes
- **Alphabets and numbers**
- **Border**

tip

If the house picture, photo or sketch that you are working from is the size you want for the finished design, it can be traced directly on to graphed tracing paper or graph paper. If it is too large or too small, enlarge or reduce it as described on page 18.

Step 2

Begin to gather the motifs together for all the items on your list, starting with the house. As each design on your list is completed, colour it in, cut it out and put it in an envelope for safe keeping until you are ready to arrange all your ingredients on the master sheet.

The House

Even if it is not a thing of great architectural beauty, the family home is an important part of our lives and deserves to be made the focal point of a house and family sampler. Unless you live in Buckingham Palace or the White House, you are not likely to find a ready-made chart of your home and you will have to draw it on to graph paper yourself. A watercolour painting of my home (shown on page 54) was used as the basis of my design, but a photograph or sketch would have done just as well. I traced the house from the painting, lining up as many vertical and horizontal lines as possible before starting to trace. The tracing was then squared up as described on page 18. When the house looked recognisably like home it was copied from the graphed tracing paper on to ordinary graph paper, coloured in, cut out and put to one side to await the rest of the ingredients.

'Apple End' is a house in the woods, hence the border of leaves and woodland creatures. The owners' initials have been included, also their cats, and an apple core to represent the name of the house.

MAKING A SKETCH

If you have no painting or photograph from which to work, you will need to make a sketch of your house. This is not as daunting as it sounds as most houses consist of straight lines, which makes them easy to draw.

- Stand square-on in front of the house and, to avoid as many awkward angles as possible, draw only one plane of the house. Be prepared for curious stares from passers-by as you do this!

- When you have a sketch showing all the details and with windows, doors, walls and roof correctly spaced in relation to each other, put your sketch on to graph paper. If you have no graphed tracing paper, draw the house to the size you want straight on to the graph paper referring to your sketch or photo.

Doors

Square up the drawing or tracing of the house, starting with the door. Find the smallest detail you want to show; you may have a much-prized door knocker so allow at least one square for this and draw the door around it to the correct proportions. Examples of doors and windows are charted on page 125. When you have drawn your door, add the porch, if you have one.

Windows

Draw in the windows, getting the proportions and spacing between them as accurate as the graph paper allows. Depending on the size of your design, you can allow one line of squares for glazing bars between panes of glass, or, if this makes your windows too large, draw the glazing bars in as backstitch lines. Backstitch can also be used to suggest leaded lights. Circular windows can be drawn using a combination of full and three-quarter cross stitch. Curtains and blinds are easily added, pot plants and cats can sit on window sills, and all help to make the house recognisable (see 'Apple End', opposite). Look carefully at your windows and see which details can be added to make it look more like home. Now draw in the side walls and the ground line. Keep checking to ensure that the proportions and spacing look right.

tip

Remember, the more detail you want to include, the larger your design will have to be. The size can be kept down if details such as door knockers, handles and letter boxes can be later sewn in backstitch and French knots.

Details

You can now add other details that make the house look like home. Window boxes, tubs of flowers, hanging baskets, lanterns and steps are just a few details that help to distinguish your home from your neighbour's, especially if you live in a row of houses all built to the same design – see the Motif Library, particularly pages 118–119. Indicate backstitch and French knots on your chart for small details and climbing plants. Draw out the name of the house if you plan to include it.

The Family

Family members can appear as figures taken from the Motif Library, or can be figures dressed in clothes to indicate their occupations. The latter was the approach chosen for the design of my own family. To represent my father, the figure of the hospital doctor in the Motif Library was turned into a family doctor by changing the white coat for a suit. My mother was a nurse and the figure in the Motif Library needed no alteration. My sister appears in her school uniform, and is the basic female figure with the addition of a school pill-box hat, blazer and pleated skirt. The figure in the teacher's academic cap and gown represents me.

Alternatively, family names can be used instead of figures. Accompany each name with a relevant symbol. If this is the method you prefer, first choose the alphabet you are going to use for the names. Draw out the names on to strips of graph paper and then draw out an appropriate symbol from the Motif Library to accompany each name.

tip

Many occupations can be found in the Motif Library as figures dressed for work. If your chosen occupation has no distinctive clothing, or you have already used figures from the Motif Library, or you do not want to use figures at all, you can use the tools of the trade or even the place of work, to represent an occupation.

Roof

Roofs in cross stitch embroidery can rise straight up in two parallel lines, or in a series of small steps converging towards the top. A gentler slope can be achieved by using the off-setting technique described on page 20. Roofs can also rise at an angle of 45° if three-quarter cross stitches are used. Study the roofs in this chapter and on page 124 and choose whichever method best suits your house. Thatch can be suggested by the use of colour and backstitch detail, as can slates or tiles. Don't forget to add the chimney, if you have one.

Work

The occupations of my family members were portrayed by dressing the family in the clothing appropriate to the occupation of each person, and in the case of my father by also making him carry the tools of the trade. The serpent twining around the staff was included as an extra medical symbol for my parents' professions, and also because there was an awkward gap to fill, and the symbol balanced well in shape and colour with the leek.

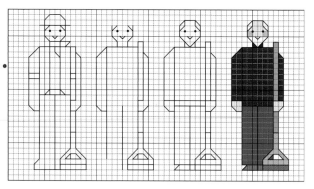

Q: How do I change a figure?

The Motif Library may have just the figure you want, or you can alter one of the figures to suit your needs, as shown in Fig 1.

1 Copy out the figure closest to your needs.

2 Erase those features you do not want.

3 Draw in the new details, which can be taken from another figure.

4 Using coloured pencils, colour in your new figure.

Fig 1 Changing a figure

Interests

Raid the Motif Library for symbols to represent the interests and hobbies on your list of ingredients. For some subjects there is more than one alternative from which to choose and your choice will depend on the prominence you want to give the symbol and on the space available. For example, a piano could have been chosen to represent 'music' on my sampler, but it would have been over large compared to the other motifs, so some bars of music were chosen instead.

Pets

My cat and her kittens were taken from the Motif Library and coloured appropriately. The rabbits, budgerigar and ducks came from the same source. Because we had a large number of kittens and rabbits, one kitten and one rabbit have been given a different pose to add variety to the line-up.

Garden

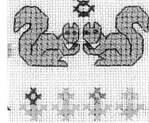

Apple blossom and butterflies were used to form my border, and other garden flowers were drawn out as small bands of flowers. The squirrels and owls, which lived in the trees in the garden, have been taken from the Motif Library, where there is a complete section on gardens. See also the summer and winter garden samplers on pages 62–63 for ideas.

Location

The county of Herefordshire in England has been represented in my sampler by cider apples and a jar of cider. The Hereford bull was adapted from the bull in the Motif Library. You might choose to show the location of your house by means of a well-known local landmark, in which case postcards are very helpful.

Nationalities

My family connections with Canada, Ireland and Wales are represented by the maple leaf, the shamrock and the leek, all taken from the Motif Library. The French and Spanish flags represent my previous occupation as a language teacher. See the Motif Library for further help and motifs.

tip

There are many different animals and breeds in the Motif Library so, hopefully, you will find your pet there. If not, follow the advice on page 112 to create your own animal design.

Alphabet and Numbers

The inclusion of an alphabet and numbers provides a link with the old tradition of sampler making. Because of the age of the house in my sampler a traditional alphabet was chosen (charted on page 140); a more modern house might look better if an alphabet that includes three-quarter cross stitch were used. Both upper case and lower case alphabets are traditionally sewn on samplers but if you do not have room for both, use the upper case (capital) letters. Draw out your chosen alphabet on to long strips of graph paper, which will be cut to size later. Add a few small flowers and hearts to the end of the strips; these will be used later to fill any gaps that are left when the alphabet is fitted inside the border. Draw out the numbers from 1 to 10; you may not have room for them all when you come to the assembly stage, or you may need to draw out more later.

Step 3

Now that you have gathered together all the motifs you plan to use in your sampler you can design the border.

Q: How do I choose a suitable border?

When choosing a border for your house and family design you might like to make it personal in some way. Whatever you choose, follow the instructions on borders on page 21, and draw out your pattern on to four long strips of graph paper, approximately to the length you think you will need.
• The name of the house or the street that it is in might suggest a theme, for example Cherry Cottage or Beehive Hill.
• Perhaps a border could be formed from a symbol on your list.
• You could use a favourite flower – see Motif Library for ideas.

Border

The size of my sampler design allowed me to use quite a wide border, and inner and outer black retaining lines were added in cross stitch to match the black timbers on the house. The colours in your border should echo the colours used somewhere in your central design. Both the apple blossom and the butterflies are in the Motif Library.

Step 4

At this stage your envelope should be bulging with drawings, each coloured in and cut out neatly. You are now ready to start arranging them on your master sheet.

Assembling the Chart

The most usual arrangement is to put your alphabet and numbers at the top of the design, with your house centrally two-thirds of the way down, and arrange the rest of the material in the remaining space. But you may have your own unique formula, so try different layouts until you find one that pleases you.

When the work is finished, sign and date it for future generations, who will have fun deciphering all your symbols. If these are very obscure, write out an explanation that can be stuck to the back of the frame to put the curious out of their misery!

SPOTTING DESIGN ERRORS

Some common errors are easily made at this stage – the following points should help you spot mistakes and rectify them

• Be prepared to be flexible; discard material that is causing problems because of size or unsuitability. Avoid cramming the design material into the space in a disorganized manner.

• Does everything balance well, or is one side fuller than the other? Is the whole design top heavy?

• Check that the overall design is the right shape to balance the ingredients, particularly the house. If your house is wider than it is tall (as a bungalow often is), a wide, landscape-shaped format would be better than a tall, portrait shape.

• Don't position the house too high up, making the design top heavy.

It is better to have it about two-thirds of the way down and, if anything, for the design to err on the side of being bottom heavy.

• Don't over-clutter the design; look at the spaces around the drawings as well as the drawings themselves. Do areas of the design need separating from each other by means of a small band of flowers or a twisted ribbon? This can have the effect of organizing the motifs into defined areas, rather than just a hotchpotch floating around in space.

• Place animals or other side-facing motifs facing into the picture, rather than out, as this draws the eye into the design.

• Check the alphabet and numbers to see if any have been left out, or if the spacing could be improved. Are you happy with the colours used?

• Decide if any small 'fillers' are needed to fill gaps. Often a flower or two, or a heart, are sufficient.

• Check that the border is correctly positioned around the design and that the corners join up correctly. Is there sufficient space between the border and the alphabet or the other motifs used?

• Check that none of your ingredients are missing or that drawings haven't disappeared into the vacuum cleaner!

Family Album

Family Album

Stitch count 102h x 90w
Design size 18.5 x 16.5cm
(7¼ x 6½in)
Fabric 28-count cream or
off-white evenweave
(or a 14-count Aida)

Use sufficient fabric to cover the
album – see page 99. Work over two
fabric threads (or one block of Aida),
using two strands of stranded cotton
for full and three-quarter cross stitches
following the chart on page 66. Work
French knots and backstitches with
one strand.

tip

Throughout the book you will
find many different styles of clothing,
headgear, footwear and hairstyles.
All are interchangeable, allowing
you to create your own character.
Take the hairstyle from one figure,
the clothing from another, add
spectacles if appropriate
and a new figure will appear.

Designing your own house and family
sampler is engrossing and rewarding
but if you prefer to concentrate on
the people in your family, the simple
house shown on the cover of the
album opposite would be a perfect
'container'. The figures in this design
can be replaced with members of
your own family for a more personal
album cover – see page 58 for advice
on changing the look of a figure.

Once you have changed the
figures to your liking, cut them out
and overlap them in the available
space to make a family group.
Finally, add your family name using
the alphabet charted on page 67.
Alternatively, you can stitch the
design as it appears in the chart. See
page 99 for making up as an album.

PERFECT BACKSTITCH

This design uses lots of backstitch –
perfect for practising this stitch.

- For neat, correct backstitch,
  don't take short cuts. You may
  be tempted to work as shown
  in Fig 2a – out at 1 and in at 2,
  out at 1 and in at 3, out at 4 and
  in at 3, out of 4 and in at 5 and
  so on. But although you may
  appear to be saving thread this
  way, you are not backstitching
  and every other stitch will be a
  long one.

- Follow Fig 2b for the correct
  sequence.

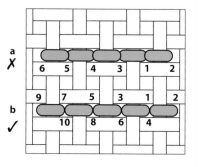

Fig 2 Backstitch working order – the
wrong way and the right way

Garden Samplers

Keen gardeners may be more inspired to immortalize their plot than their house, and the same principles can be followed when designing a sampler showing aspects of your garden. The two samplers shown here represent a garden in summer and in winter, with normal perspective mixed with bird's-eye views to create interesting and colourful designs.

Samplers like these lend themselves well to being worked with additional decorative stitches, and so give you the opportunity to experiment. See overleaf for the charts. You could also change some of the motifs used – search the Motif Library for ideas.

Summer and Winter Garden Samplers

Stitch count 96h x 83w

Design size 17.5 x 15cm
(6¾ x 6in)

Fabric 28-count country style
evenweave (or a 14-count Aida)

Work over two fabric threads (or one block of Aida), using two strands of stranded cotton for full and three-quarter cross stitches following the charts overleaf. Work French knots and backstitches with one strand.

Summer Garden
Cross stitch

	DMC		DMC		DMC		DMC		DMC
•	blanc	■	321		415		701	—	738
	209	II	352		433		703	2	798
	301		353	+	604	/	720		809
■	310	O	414	9	699		726		938

Backstitch
	DMC
⊂⊃	blanc
—	310
—	701

French knots
	DMC
🌀	310
🌀	701
🌀	726

Winter Garden
Cross stitch

DMC				
• blanc	316	○ 414	701	798
301	4 321	415	720	809
307	II 352	433	738	
⊡ 310	353	699	796	

Backstitch
DMC
- ══ blanc
- ━━ 310
- ━━ 433
- ━━ 701
- ━━ 720

French knots
DMC
- 🌀 blanc
- 🌀 310
- 🌀 699

Chart background
shown as pale blue
to show white cross
stitches more clearly

Family Album
Cross stitch
DMC

· blanc	554	✳ 761	966
334	604	762	3811
552	754	839	3822

Backstitch
DMC

— 762
— 310

French knots
DMC

♥ 310

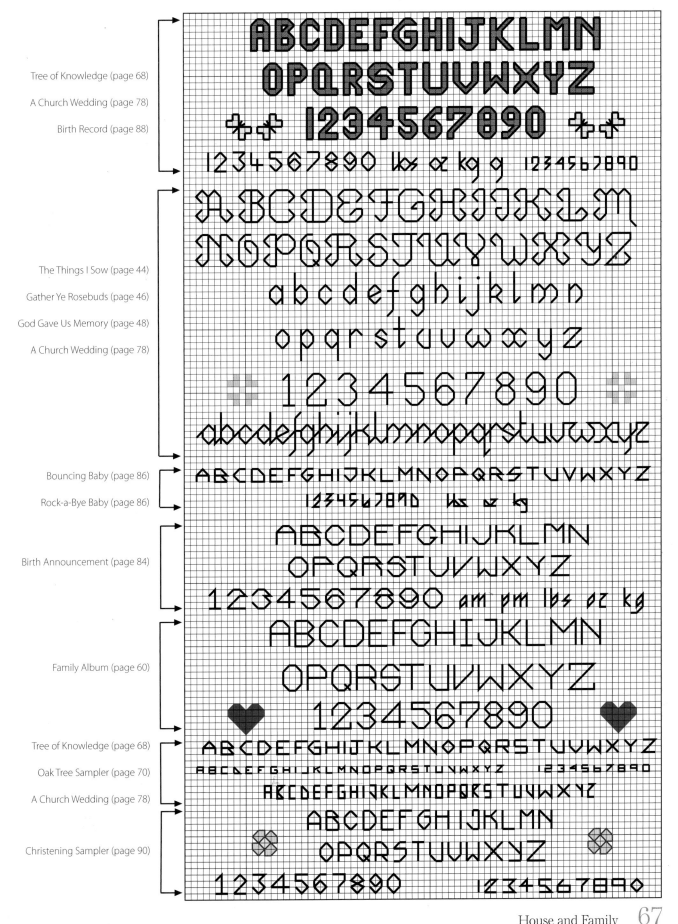

Family Trees

One of the commonest symbols to be found on old samplers is the tree.

Representing life, strength and fruitfulness, it appears in many stylized forms

and has been revered by many cultures. Three family tree samplers are shown

in this chapter, with advice on how to adapt them for your own family.

Family Tree Samplers

Whichever of the three family tree designs you chose to stitch from this chapter, when you have sewn it you will have a decorative and durable record of your family history.

The Tree of Knowledge sampler, shown opposite, shows the Verso family tree. The apple tree and serpent in the Garden of Eden is flanked by Adam and Eve. The chart on pages 74–75 can be adapted to depict your family tree and be surrounded by many symbols (see overleaf for some symbols with traditional meanings).

The Oak Tree sampler (shown on page 71 and charted on page 76) represents the strength of family bonds and can be adapted quite easily to suit your family.

The Apple Family Tree (shown on page 73 and charted on page 77), has a simple structure, with a line-up of family members that can be adapted to reflect your family.

Tree of Knowledge Sampler

You could work the design as it is charted, backstitching the names of your family into the spaces provided using the alphabet on page 67.

Adapting the Sampler

You may prefer to adjust the design to portray your own family. If creating your own design, read the instructions on pages 22–23, and then follow the steps below.

1 On separate slips of graph paper, write out the names of each family member using the alphabet of your choice (see pages 67, 140 and 142). For long names choose a tiny alphabet. Add dates of birth if you wish and have the space.

2 Draw out one large apple per person. Copy out the trunk of the tree with Adam and Eve on either side of it and then copy out the cherubs and the crown (representing a marriage made in heaven).

3 Copy out several branches to fill any gaps between the names when you come to arrange them. Copy out the pointed tree top.

4 Copy out two garlands and fill each with an appropriate initial (alphabet on page 67). A garland symbolizes eternal love, going round and round without end.

5 Select two traditional symbols from page 127 that have some relevance to your family and copy them out.

6 Copy out eight long apple and leaf border strips to the approximate size you think you will need, with eight large apples to go in the corners and in the centre of each side.

7 Take a sheet of graph paper large enough to hold the complete design (the master sheet), and arrange all your symbols on it, using the chart on pages 74–75 for general guidance. Depending on the shape of your tree you may have other gaps that can be filled with hearts, flowers, dates or other symbols.

8 If the border needs enlarging, lengthen the apple and leaf strips by adding more pattern repeats. If the strips are too long, shorten them by removing the necessary number of apples and leaves. When happy with the spacing and arrangement of all the material, draw an inner and outer retaining line around the border to complete the picture.

9 Follow steps 3 and 4 on page 23 to prepare the master sheet for stitching.

Tree of Knowledge Sampler

Stitch count 126h x 110w
Design size 23 x 20cm (9 x 7¾in)
Fabric 28-count antique white evenweave (or a 14-count Aida)

Work over two fabric threads (or one block of Aida), using two strands of stranded cotton for full and three-quarter cross stitches, following the chart on pages 74–75. Work French knots and backstitches with one strand.

TRADITIONAL SYMBOLS AND THEIR MEANINGS

There are many symbols used in embroidery and a few have been selected for the designs in this chapter, charted on page 127 of the Motif Library.

Rose the flower of love

Basket of fruit fertility and fruitfulness

Dog fidelity

Two doves facing concord

Dove with an olive branch peace and charity

Owl wisdom

Peacock vanity, luxury and ostentation

Bee hope and industriousness

Hour glass the transience of life

Anchor steadfastness

Swan the bird of love

Heart love

Squirrel mischief

Butterfly joy, inconstancy

Bunch of grapes Christ

Key the key to the kingdom of Heaven

Candle prayer

Beehive monastic or other community

Oak Tree Sampler

If you want to stitch a simple family tree you could work the design as it is charted on page 76, placing the names of your family members into the spaces provided using the backstitch alphabet on page 67.

Oak Tree Sampler

Stitch count	125h x 99w
Design size	23 x 18cm (9 x 7in)
Fabric	28-count cream or off-white evenweave (or a 14-count Aida)

Work over two fabric threads (or one block of Aida), using two strands of stranded cotton for full and three-quarter cross stitches following the chart on page 76. Work French knots and backstitches with one strand.

tip
Arrange the names with the oldest generation at the top and the youngest at the bottom. Where one line of the family finishes and another continues, fill the gap with an owl or squirrel perched in the tree.

Adapting the Sampler
To adjust and rearrange the design to portray your own family, follow the steps below after reading the instructions in Designing a Sampler on pages 22–23.

1 On separate slips of graph paper draw out the names of each family member using the alphabet of your choice. For long names choose a very tiny alphabet (see pages 67, 140 and 142). Add their dates of birth if using them and have room. Draw out one acorn per person.

2 Depending on the size of your proposed tree, draw out a number of oak leaves facing to the right and a number facing to the left.

3 Copy out the trunk of the tree, together with the toadstools, squirrel and badger. If you prefer other animals, substitute them – more animals can be found in the Motif Library.

4 Draw out four long border strips of acorns and oak leaves to the approximate length you think you will need.

5 Take a sheet of graph paper large enough to hold the complete design (the master sheet), and arrange all your symbols on it, using the chart on page 76 for general guidance.

6 If the border needs enlarging, add extra acorns and oak leaves to the strips. If the border needs reducing, cut off as many acorns and oak leaves as necessary. Check that you are happy with the arrangement of acorns or oak leaves in the four corners. When you are happy with the spacing and arrangement of all the design material, draw an inner and outer retaining line around the border to complete the picture.

7 Now follow steps 3 and 4 on page 23 to prepare your family tree master sheet for stitching.

Apple Family Tree

Stitch count	66h x 64w
Design size	12 x 11.5cm
	(4¾ x 4½in)
Fabric	27-count Zweigart
	Linda evenweave in
	antique white
	(or a 14-count Aida)

Work over two fabric threads (or one block of Aida), using two strands of stranded cotton for full and three-quarter cross stitches following the chart on page 77. Work French knots and backstitches with one strand.

Apple Family Tree

Three generations are represented on this family tree, which is adaptable to suit everybody's circumstances. Simply change the initials to suit the family history using the alphabet supplied with the chart. Photocopy the design and draw the required initials in the spaces on the chart. Place the grandparents' initials on the top line, the parents' on the second and the child's initials on the bottom line.

The attractive border is composed of apples at various stages of maturity to reflect the different ages pictured on the family tree. Subtle colour variations have been achieved by employing a useful technique called 'tweeding' – see the feature below.

Depicting Character Details

The people portrayed at the bottom of the design can be altered to look more like the people in your family. Height, hair colour and style, and clothing can all be altered as necessary, and jewellery jump rings can be stitched to faces for spectacle wearers. The Motif Library has many figures with different styles of clothing, footwear, hairstyles, hats and so on. See also Fig 1 on page 58, which describes how to change a figure.

Q: How do I tweed threads?

The ripening apples in the border are worked with two different shades of stranded cotton. Where orange, for example, changes to yellow a row of 'tweeding' is worked to soften the transition and give a more natural effect. This is achieved quite simply by working the stitches with one strand of orange thread and one strand of yellow thread together in the needle. The rest of the two-toned apples are worked in the same way, using the shades given in the chart key. You can also tweed different types of threads together, say a stranded cotton and a shiny rayon, or a cotton with a metallic thread.

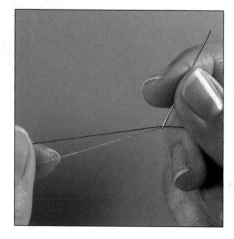

1 Thread the needle with the two different colour threads.

2 Work full and three-quarter cross stitches with the mixed colour thread.

3 Finish stitching the two-tone apple and carefully outline it in backstitch.

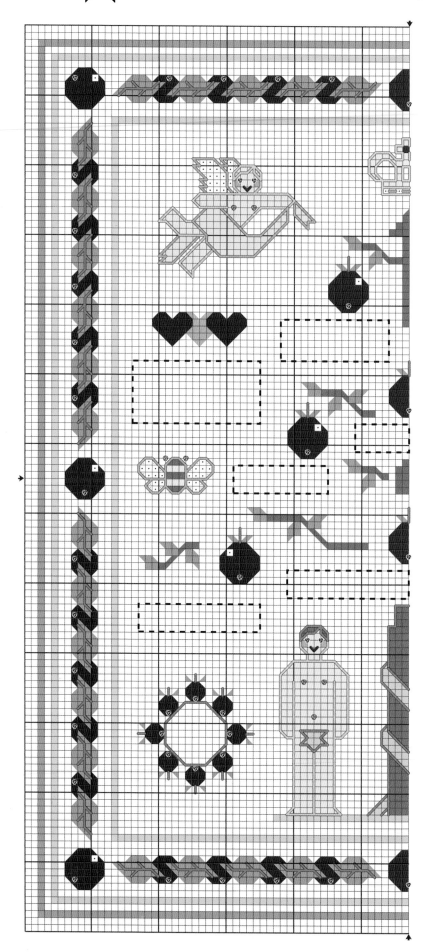

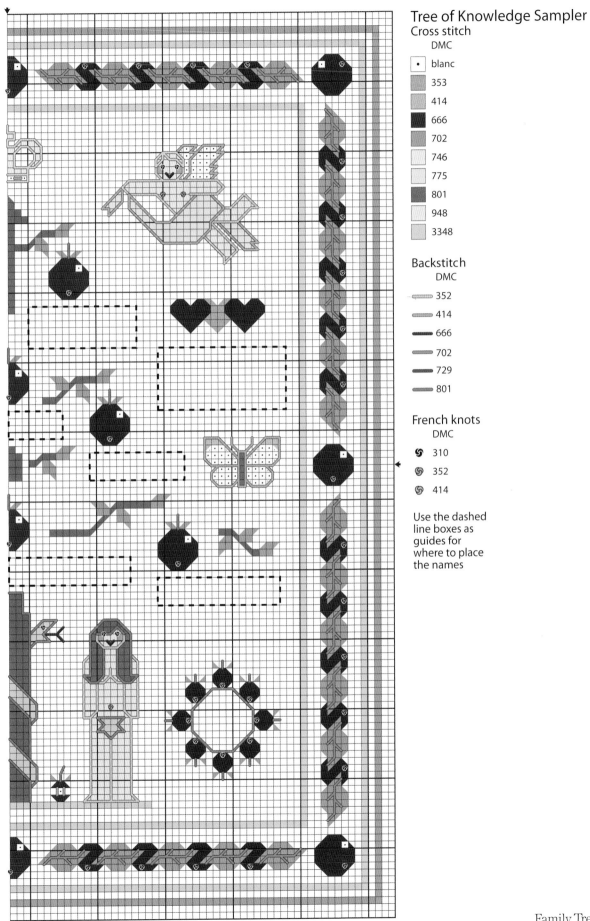

Tree of Knowledge Sampler

Cross stitch

DMC

•	blanc
	353
	414
	666
	702
	746
	775
	801
	948
	3348

Backstitch

DMC

	352
	414
	666
	702
	729
	801

French knots

DMC

✿	310
✿	352
✿	414

Use the dashed line boxes as guides for where to place the names

Oak Tree Sampler

Cross stitch
DMC

•	blanc
⊙	310
	415
◇	470
	471
✳	472
⊖	581
	701
	741
	869
	904
	922

Backstitch
DMC

——	310
——	869
——	918

French knots
DMC

⟳	blanc
⟳	310

Place an initial either side of the French knots

Apple Family Tree
Cross stitch

	DMC						
•	blanc		445		704		797
	300		498		742		809
	310	△	700		746		946
	318		702	↗	754		948

1 strand each of:
DMC

✳ 445 + 742
↖ 704 + 445
⊞ 742 + 946

Backstitch
DMC

— 310
— 498
— 797

French knots
DMC

❡ 310

Love and Marriage

Weddings, engagements and anniversaries are all great family occasions to be recorded and celebrated in cross stitch. In a wedding sampler, a traditional approach includes hearts, flowers and lovebirds, and perhaps the names and a date. A more adventurous approach is possible by adding the figures of the people involved and the location.

A Church Wedding

The sampler shown opposite records my first marriage. A border of flowers and bows was used as bows can represent 'tying the knot'. Wedding bells are included in the border at the top and intertwined wedding rings at the bottom. The church in one corner is balanced by the wedding cake in the other. The bride and the groom stand in the church doorway with guests and bridesmaids on either side. The date is included, with the name of the church and the time of the wedding. Two garlands contain the bride's and groom's initials. Small gaps are filled with rows of hearts and other wedding symbols.

tip
Don't overdo details on the bride or she will look cluttered. Choose the most important details rather than adding every last button and bead. A wedding photograph is a useful aid to memory.

Adapting the Sampler

My sampler is easily adapted to suit your own wedding. Before you begin, read the general instructions on pages 22–23. Various wedding motifs and wedding figures are charted in the Motif Library.

1 Start by drawing out your own church, following a similar procedure to drawing a house (see page 56). A photograph is useful, or make a sketch of the church.

2 Draw out the wedding cake with the appropriate number of tiers. Add a large cake stand if you need extra height to balance with your church, or place a bottle of champagne and some glasses beside it to add extra width if necessary.

3 Draw out the bride, changing the headdress, veil, hair style, dress and bouquet as necessary. Use backstitch and French knots for small details. Draw the groom, making any necessary changes or additions, such as a beard or spectacles. If he wore a uniform, replace the morning suit with as accurate a uniform as possible. Stand the groom next to the bride and draw out the doorway of the church around them. If your doorway differs greatly from the arch in the basic pattern you could re-draw it.

4 Draw bridesmaids and pages, adding the appropriate clothing or using the figures as a starting point and making the necessary changes. Adjust the height of the figures to show differing ages.

5 Add the parents of the couple, the guests, the best man and the officiating priest to the line-up. Use figures from the Motif Library, giving them recognisable clothing and headgear.

6 Using the alphabet of your choice, draw out the wedding date, together with other wording you wish to include. Copy out two garlands and fill each with an initial from the alphabet on page 67.

7 Draw out four long border strips, one containing the wedding bells for the top, one with wedding rings for the bottom, and two side strips. Alternatively, draw another border of your choice.

8 Take a sheet of graph paper large enough to hold the complete design (the master sheet), and arrange all your motifs on it, using the sampler photograph for general guidance.

9 If the border needs enlarging, add extra pattern repeats; if you need a smaller border simply cut off the necessary number of repeats. When you are happy with the spacing and arrangement of all the design material, draw an inner line and a double outer retaining line around the border to complete the picture.

10 Follow steps 3 and 4, page 23 to prepare the master for stitching.

A Registry Office Wedding

Registry Office weddings can be celebrated in embroidery just as effectively as church weddings but with a few changes of approach. You could create a design with a romantic border of hearts and flowers, and with church bells replaced by two intertwined wedding rings. A standard porch entrance could be used instead of the arch of a church doorway. Space could be left above the door for you to include the name of the registry office where the wedding took place. Stand the bride and groom in the doorway dressed in their finery, with guests on either side. Leave space on both sides for the addition of the couples' names. Place the wedding date at the top, together with two garlands filled with appropriate initials. For good luck, add horseshoes and white heather to complete the picture.

Wedding Gifts and Cards

Three smaller projects have been included in this chapter, each with their own chart. All are simple to stitch and make lovely keepsakes of the special occasion. Two pretty wedding card designs have been stitched and mounted into ready-made cards, one in a gothic-shaped aperture (see below). A beautiful ring pillow (opposite) decorated with a lace trim, ribbons and roses will ensure that the wedding rings are kept safe.

Ring Pillow

Stitch count	53h x 46w
Design size	10.2 x 9cm (4 x 3½in)
Fabric	27-count Zweigart Linda evenweave in cream (or a 14-count Aida)

Work over two fabric threads (or one block of Aida), using two strands of stranded cotton for full and three-quarter cross stitches following the chart on page 83. Work French knots and backstitches with one strand. Sew on the seed beads with a beading needle and matching thread. Stitch the names and dates beside and below the heart design. Make up the ring pillow as described on page 98.

Church Wedding Card

Stitch count	53h x 27w
Design size	10.2 x 5cm (4 x 2in)
Fabric	27-count Zweigart Linda evenweave in cream (or a 14-count Aida)

Dove Wedding Card

Stitch count	29h x 44w
Design size	5.5 x 8.5cm (2¼ x 3½in)
Fabric	27-count Zweigart Oslo Hardanger in cream (or a 14-count Aida)

Work over two fabric threads (or one block of Aida), using two strands of stranded cotton for full and three-quarter cross stitches following the relevant chart on page 83. Work French knots and backstitches with one strand. Use the alphabet provided to stitch the initials or use the alphabet on page 67. See page 97 for making up a card. Trim the cards as shown or with embellishments of your choice.

WEDDING ANNIVERSARIES

Whether you are designing a card or a more ambitious picture, the motifs on pages 128 and 129 could be helpful. Follow the instructions on designs previously given to produce a unique piece of embroidery to celebrate the occasion. The list of wedding anniversaries provided below will give you some ideas on trimmings you might use for wedding gifts and cards.

- For a Silver Wedding (25 years) consider using silver wedding bells, silver horseshoes, a cake with the number 25 written on it, or even an enlarged cake with 25 candles. You may wish to represent the church where the couple were married, or to include symbols from the Motif Library that are of relevance to the life they have lived together.

- For a Golden Wedding (50 years), substitute golden motifs, a cake with 50 written on it and use gold thread for the wording.

- Ruby (40) or Emerald Weddings (55) could use red or green in the border; the engagement ring charted on page 128 can become a ruby or emerald ring if sewn with ruby- or emerald-coloured thread.

- The 'Happy Anniversary' roundel on page 128 could be altered to fit any anniversary – just change the colour of the hearts and use the alphabet and numbers on page 67 to change the details of the anniversary.

The design would make a perfect card to celebrate the special occasion, or become part of a larger sampler. The following trimmings might be used.

1st Paper
Paper flowers or petal-type confetti

2nd Cotton
Miniature cotton reels or cotton thread wound round small card bobbins

3rd Leather
Leather-look buttons

4th Fruit
Fruit-shaped beads or buttons

5th Wood
Wooden beads or buttons

6th Sugar or Candy
Sugar cubes or sweets

7th Wool
Woollen pompons or a small toy sheep

8th Bronze
Coins

9th Pottery
Miniature pot or dolls' house flower pot

10th Tin
Any tin-coloured shiny trinket or dolls' house food tins

11th Steel
Steel beads or darning needles

12th Silk
Silk flowers or silk thread wound around small card bobbins

13th Lace
Miniature lace bobbins or guipure lace flower motifs

14th Ivory
Use an elephant pendant rather than anything made of ivory

15th Crystal
Clear faceted beads

16th China
China beads or doll's house cups

25th Silver
Silver charms, coins or rings

30th Pearl
Pearl beads or buttons

35th Coral
Coral beads

40th Ruby
Red faceted beads or a red heart pendant

45th Sapphire
Blue faceted beads

50th Gold
Rings, beads or any golden trinkets

55th Emerald
Green faceted beads

60th Diamond
Glass faceted beads

Engagements

Having read through this chapter and those preceding it, you will see how a very personal record of an occasion can be put together. A greetings card offering congratulations to an engaged couple can be concocted from the designs of an engagement ring, a champagne bottle and good luck symbols (see page 128). See pages 67, 140 and 142 for alphabets you could use. The couple themselves could also be included, using figures from the Motif Library, and their occupations and interests may be found in the same source. A larger picture could be produced. Hearts, flowers, love birds, names, dates and figures are all grist to your mill and can be used to create a memorable and most acceptable gift.

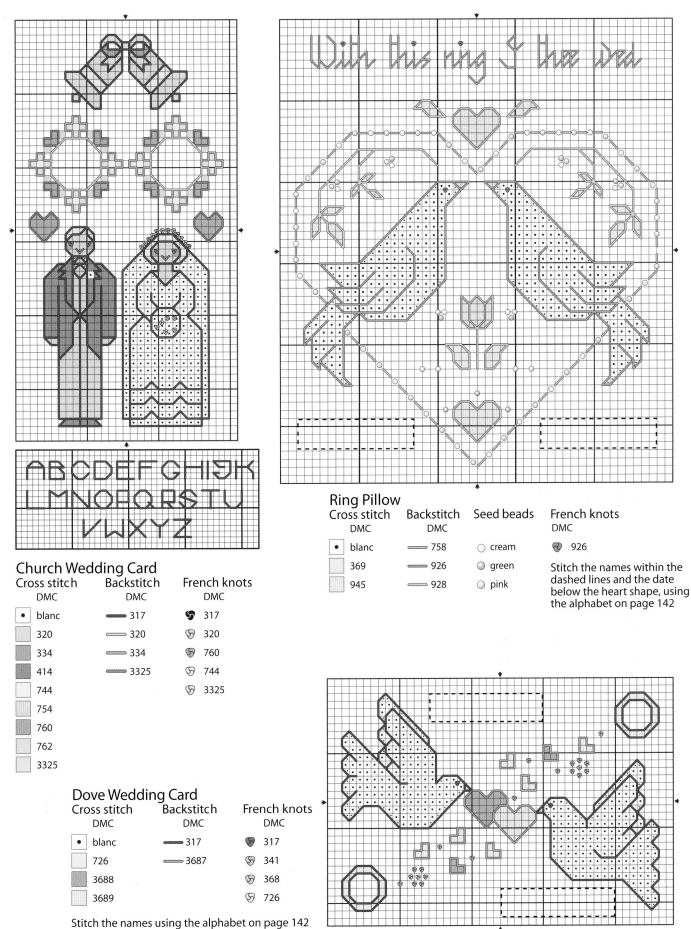

Church Wedding Card

Cross stitch	Backstitch	French knots
DMC	DMC	DMC
• blanc	—— 317	317
320	—— 320	320
334	—— 334	760
414	—— 3325	744
744		3325
754		
760		
762		
3325		

Dove Wedding Card

Cross stitch	Backstitch	French knots
DMC	DMC	DMC
• blanc	—— 317	317
726	—— 3687	341
3688		368
3689		726

Stitch the names using the alphabet on page 142

Ring Pillow

Cross stitch	Backstitch	Seed beads	French knots
DMC	DMC		DMC
• blanc	—— 758	○ cream	926
369	—— 926	○ green	
945	—— 928	○ pink	

Stitch the names within the dashed lines and the date below the heart shape, using the alphabet on page 142

Birth and Babies

What better excuse could there be to reach for your needle than the arrival of a new baby? This chapter has a charming design for a birth announcement (shown opposite), a fun birth record, a christening sampler and two pretty cards, which can all be stitched following their charts or be adapted to suit you.

Birth Announcement

Stitch count 80h x 56w
Design size 14.5 x 10.2cm
(5¾ x 4in)
Fabric 27-count Zweigart
Linda evenweave
in ivory
(or a 14-count Aida)

Work over two fabric threads (or one block of Aida), using two strands of stranded cotton for full and three-quarter cross stitches following the chart on page 87. Work French knots and backstitches with one strand. To add the name and other details, use the alphabet and numbers on page 67. Draw the name out on graph paper to find the centre point. Line this up with the centre point of the top border so there are equal spaces on either side. Stick the name into position on the chart. Now add the date, time of arrival and the baby's weight in the same way.

Birth Announcement

The birth sampler shown opposite makes a lovely framed picture but it could also be used on a photograph album. The stork was out on another call, so this baby baled out and found a novel method of delivery! Use this design to record for posterity the birth details of a new baby, adding the name, date, time and weight using the alphabet and numbers charted on page 67 or another alphabet of your choice. You could omit the flowers at the top if the name you are using is a longer one.

New Arrival Cards

Welcome a new addition to the family with these pretty cards (shown here and overleaf), or create your own card designs using motifs and alphabets from the Motif Library. See page 97 for mounting work into cards and making your own cards.

tip
Four of the parachute strings on Birth Announcement do not descend at 45°. When stitching these it's helpful to lay a strand of tacking thread tautly between the two points to be joined, as a guide for backstitching. Remove the thread when the strings are complete.

Rock-a-Bye Baby Card (left)

Stitch count 47h x 43w

Design size 8.5 x 7.6cm
(3½ x 3in)

Fabric 27-count Zweigart
Linda evenweave
in cream

Bouncing Baby Card (page 84)

Stitch count 48h x 42w

Design size 8.5 x 7.6cm
(3½ x 3in)

Fabric 27-count Zweigart
Linda evenweave
in cream

Work over two fabric threads (or one block of 14-count Aida), using two strands of stranded cotton for full and three-quarter cross stitches. Work French knots and backstitches with one strand. To add the name and other details, backstitch within the dashed lines on the chart, using the alphabet and numbers on page 67. See page 97 for instructions on making up a card. Tie thin toning ribbon around the spine of the card or add other trims and embellishments as desired.

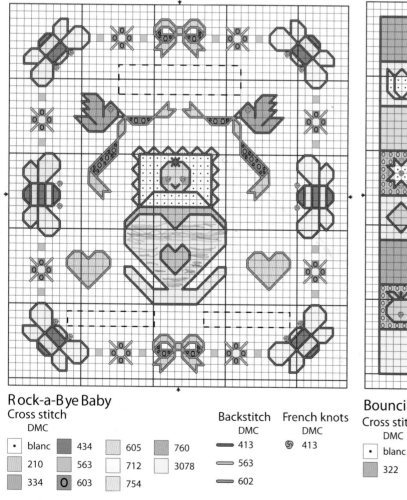

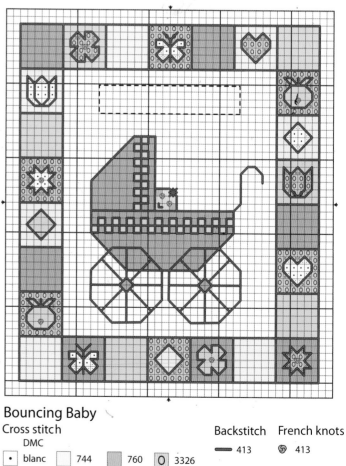

Rock-a-Bye Baby
Cross stitch
DMC

•	blanc		434		605		760
	210		563		712		3078
	334	O	603		754		

Backstitch
DMC
— 413
— 563
— 602

French knots
DMC
🌀 413

Bouncing Baby
Cross stitch
DMC

•	blanc		744		760	O	3326
	322		754		964		

Backstitch
DMC
— 413

French knots
DMC
🌀 413

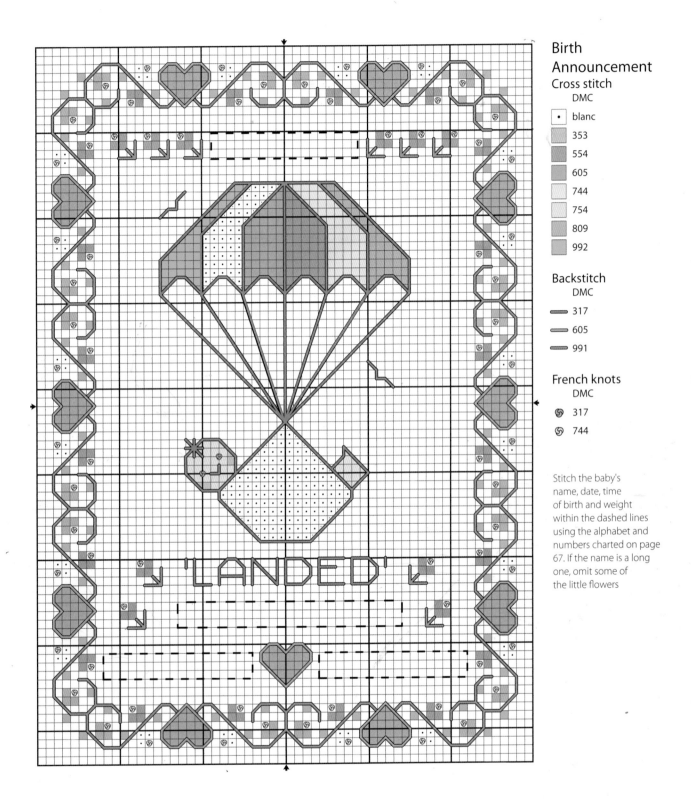

Birth Announcement

Cross stitch
DMC

- · blanc
- 353
- 554
- 605
- 744
- 754
- 809
- 992

Backstitch
DMC

- —— 317
- —— 605
- —— 991

French knots
DMC

- ⊛ 317
- ⊛ 744

Stitch the baby's name, date, time of birth and weight within the dashed lines using the alphabet and numbers charted on page 67. If the name is a long one, omit some of the little flowers

'LANDED'

Birth Record

Stitch count 74h x 63w

Design size 13.5 x 11.5cm
(5¼ x 4½in)

Fabric 28-count cream
evenweave
(or a 14-count Aida)

Work over two fabric threads (or one block of Aida), using two strands of stranded cotton for full and three-quarter cross stitches following the chart on page 92 where relevant and your own chart. Work French knots and backstitches with one strand.

Birth Record

The picture of 'Harry' shown opposite has been designed as a birth record and includes all the details of his birth sewn on to his 'patchwork quilt'. With a few simple changes the basic chart on page 92 can be made to record the birth details of any baby.

Adapting the Design

Start by reading the general design instructions in Designing a Sampler on pages 22–23, and then follow the steps below.

1 Copy the outline shape of the bed on to graph paper. Decorate it with hearts and flowers.

2 Draw in the baby's head, adding more hair if desired and then add the pillow and sheet.

3 Draw the squares on the quilt but leave them blank for the time being.

4 Draw the potty and toys to be placed under and around the bed. You may wish to create your own toy motifs.

5 Using the alphabet on page 67 draw out the name of the baby. Stick the name into place, centred on the bed.

6 Fill in the squares on the quilt with an appropriate symbol (see suggestions, left). Draw each symbol on to a separate piece of graph paper so they can be shuffled around to find the best position for each one on the quilt.

7 Colour in your design to suit your taste, your colour scheme, or the sex of the baby, making the dominant colours pink for a girl or blue for a boy if you wish.

8 Arrange the drawings of the toys around the bed following the basic pattern, or in a new arrangement to suit yourself. Arrange the symbols on the quilt and shuffle them around to get the best layout.

9 When you are satisfied with your design, stick the drawings on to the master sheet to produce your finished chart ready for stitching (see steps 3 and 4 on page 23).

SUGGESTED QUILT SYMBOLS

The coloured patches on the quilt can have whatever motifs or symbols you wish. I used the following patterns, which can be found in the Motif Library but any small symbol that seems appropriate – a heart, a butterfly, a flower – can replace any of these suggestions.

- Mother's and Father's initials from the alphabet on page 67.

- Clock to indicate the time of birth; adjust the hands to show the correct time.

- Date of birth.

- Mother's nationality, using a small flag. Substitute the height of the baby at birth if you wish.

- Birth weight of the baby.

- Father's nationality, using a small flag. Substitute the initial of a brother or sister if you wish.

- Baby's birth sign (see page 133).

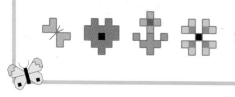

tip

If the name is too long to fit the space on the bed, omit the flowers on either side of the name. If the name still does not fit, choose a smaller alphabet or one that can be sewn in backstitch.

Christening Sampler

The christening sampler I stitched for my daughters is shown opposite and, as with the wedding designs in the previous chapter, a basic christening chart is provided for you to adapt to suit the christening you wish to record.

Christening Sampler

Stitch count	109h x 89w
Design size	20 x 16.5cm
	(7¾ x 6½in)
Fabric	28-count cream evenweave (or a 14-count Aida)

Work over two fabric threads (or one block of Aida), using two strands of stranded cotton for full and three-quarter cross stitches following the chart on page 93 where relevant and your own chart. Work French knots and backstitches with one strand.

Adapting the Sampler

Start by reading the general design instructions in Designing a Sampler on pages 22–23, and then adapt the design by following the steps below.

1 Begin with the church. You could use the basic church pattern charted on page 93, or if your church differs greatly, re-draw it using a photograph or sketch to help (see page 78 for advice). If you want to include a steeple that doesn't rise at 45º, bring the pencil up the sides in a series of small steps. Check that both sides match, and that both rise at the same pitch. Make use of the off-setting technique on page 20 to soften the stepped effect. Remember that this is cross stitch embroidery, so allow yourself some artistic licence. Identify the church by drawing out its name in the lettering of your choice. If your church has a clock on the tower you can set the hands at the time the christening took place.

2 Copy out two floral crosses to place beside the church. Draw the font, or adapt it if your font differs; add the two candles and the water pouring from the shell. Copy out two white doves to place above the font. Using the alphabet on page 67, draw out the name of the baby and the date of the christening; the word 'Christened' can be replaced with 'Baptised' if you prefer. Copy out the priest holding the baby, and make adjustments to the appearance of the priest or the christening robe to make them recognisable.

3 Draw out two parents and change their clothing and appearance to record how they looked on the day. Draw out the names of the godparents, putting a flower between each name. Copy out several bands of flowers to cut to size later to fill any gaps. Now draw out four border strips, each with a corner.

4 Arrange all your drawings on a master sheet and, using the basic pattern as a rough guide, shuffle them around to find the best arrangement. Fill any gaps with flowers, or remove flowers that have been squeezed out by the inclusion of extra design material. Check your border fits correctly around the whole design, and when colouring it in, use a light and a darker shade of the same colour to emphasize the twisting effect of the ribbon. The colour of the flowers on the border can be repeated in the floral crosses and bands of flowers. When satisfied with your layout, stick your motifs on to the master sheet.

tip

There are other approaches to representing a church. Perhaps it has a distinctive lych-gate (a roofed gateway) or other feature that could be substituted, or maybe you could do a ground plan of the church seen from a bird's-eye view. If all else fails, consider drawing the altar with its linen and candlesticks.

tip

If you have included more material than is given in the basic chart, e.g., a larger church or more figures of guests around the font, lengthen the border strips by adding extra twists of ribbon at the points where the border reverses, not in the corners.

5 When adapting the basic pattern to suit my circumstances, my two children were included in the design. Two sets of names and dates were used, so the lettering under the church was re-shuffled. Both babies had to make an appearance, so the figure of the priest holding the baby was reversed. This second priest figure was substituted for parent figures. Two babies meant two sets of godparents, so the lettering at the bottom needed rearranging. The newly created gaps were filled with flowers. The church was re-drawn in sufficient detail to make it recognisable, and its name appears above it. When embroidering the water pouring into the font, silver thread added sparkle to the occasion.

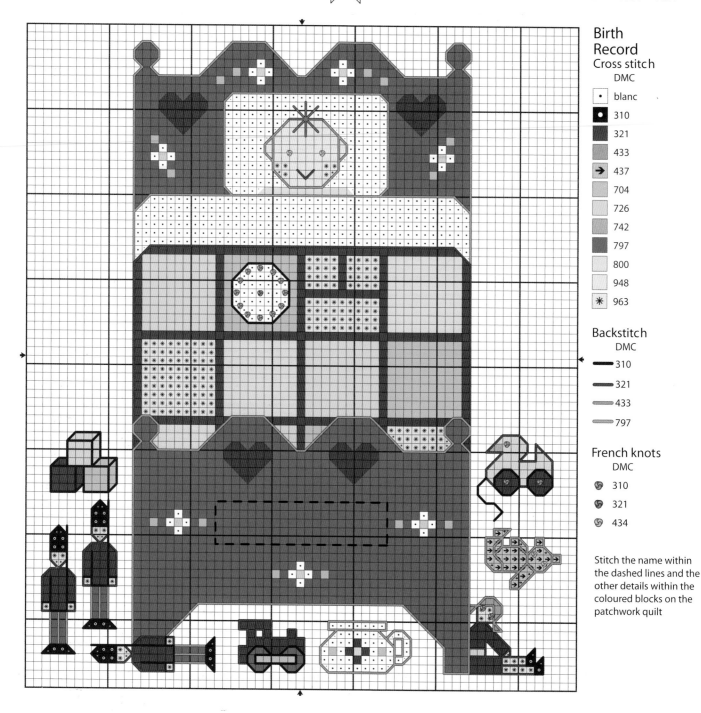

Birth Record
Cross stitch
DMC

·	blanc
⬤	310
	321
	433
→	437
	704
	726
	742
	797
	800
	948
✳	963

Backstitch
DMC

▬▬	310
▬▬	321
▬▬	433
▬▬	797

French knots
DMC

🌀	310
🌀	321
🌀	434

Stitch the name within the dashed lines and the other details within the coloured blocks on the patchwork quilt

tip
When working three-quarter cross stitch, do not pull the first stitch tight before working the quarter stitch, as this will obscure the hole into which you work the quarter stitch.

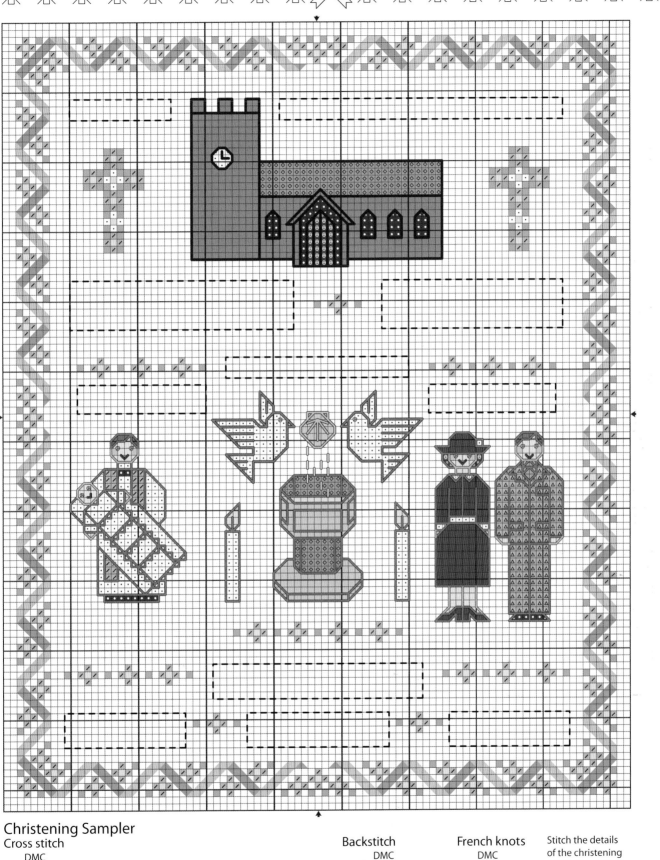

Christening Sampler

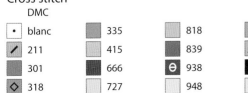

Cross stitch

DMC

• blanc	335	818	989	
∕ 211	415	839	△ 3032	
301	666	⊖ 938	● 3799	
◇ 318	727	948	metallic silver	

Backstitch

DMC

335
666
839
3799
metallic silver

French knots

DMC

🌀 839
🌀 3799

Stitch the details
of the christening
within the dashed
lines, omitting
some of the little
flowers if more
space is needed

93

Finishing and Making Up

This chapter gives advice on transforming your cross stitch embroidery into unique items you will enjoy for years. The making up techniques used in the book are explained, including how to mount and frame embroidery, how to display work in hoops, in greetings cards and on photo albums, and how to create napkin rings and little pillows.

Finishing Off

When you think that your embroidery is complete, check it to make sure that you have worked everything on your pattern, and that you have not left any part of the design unworked other than the background. If you have created a sampler, now is the time to sign and date your work, to claim it as your own and for the interest of future generations. Check that you have finished off all loose ends at the back of the work, as any stray threads lying behind unworked ground may show through when the work is mounted and spoil the look.

tip

If work is framed behind glass with any trace of moisture present, mould can cause severe problems later, producing unsightly stains on your work, which will ruin it.

Washing and Ironing Embroidery

Your finished work should be clean but if there has been some mishap you may have to wash it before it is mounted. This is to be avoided if possible, and the following instructions are for newly completed work only. (If you are contemplating washing an old or antique piece of embroidery, it is advisable to seek specialist advice before starting or the results could be disastrous.)

1 First test the threads for colour fastness. Modern threads are generally reliable, but it is better to be safe than sorry. Take extra care with strong reds. Moisten a cotton bud in tepid water and rub it over the back of the stitches. If no colour comes off on the cotton bud, it is probably safe to wash the piece.

2 Use tepid water and thoroughly dissolve some good quality soap flakes or a mild, non-biological powder in it. Whilst washing your embroidery avoid pulling or rubbing, as this will distort your stitches; a gentle swish round should be sufficient to dislodge any grime. Rinse well using several changes of tepid water – do not wring your work.

3 To dry, lay the embroidery flat on a clean white towel and leave until it is thoroughly dry.

4 If you have kept your work rolled on to a tube for storage there shouldn't be too many stubborn creases to remove. There is no need to block and stretch cross stitch embroidery as in canvas work. If a hoop or a frame has been used, a light press should be all that it needs. To press your work there is no need to dampen it. Lay a thick, fluffy white towel on a flat surface. Place your work face down on the towel and then cover it with a clean, white cotton cloth. Press gently with a warm iron, nudging the iron up to the edges of the stitching, thus only pressing the unworked fabric. If you need to press the stitching itself you can do so as the towel will allow the stitches to sink into its pile and thus avoid flattening the stitches. Heavily pressed stitching will look flat and lifeless. Avoid ironing over any beads you may have used and take extra care with metallic threads.

Mounting Embroidery

If you do not wish to have your work framed, it can be mounted on to hardboard. The hardboard needs to be covered with a clean, cotton fabric to ensure that there is no contact between it and the work. Take care to choose a cotton fabric that is plain and a colour that does not show through your embroidery. Using a strong button thread or fine cord, lace the work in place on the back of the board from side to side and from top to bottom (see Fig 1). The work will need to be removed from the board periodically for cleaning as it will not be protected by glass.

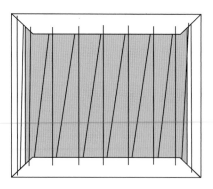

Fig 1 Lacing work on to hardboard

Framing Embroidery

Hopefully, having spent so much time and effort on your design and the embroidering of it, you will think that your work deserves expert framing to give it the professional finishing touch.

Most framers mount embroidery on to card, which is less bulky than hardboard. Check with your framer that the work will be mounted on to acid-free card. If the card is not acid free, foxing can occur, which produces unsightly brown patches after a while. Ask your framer not to allow the glass to come into contact with the stitches, as this will flatten them. Use a mount made of acid-free card to raise the glass off the work, or ask the framer to raise the glass by means of thin strips of card packed around the edge of the frame where the overlap will hide them from view. Non-reflective glass can be used, but my preference is for plain glass, which gives a clearer view of the stitches.

Consider carefully where your 'masterpiece' is to hang. Avoid hanging it in strong or direct sunlight, as this will fade the colours eventually and can also rot the fabric, but equally do not hide your work away in the gloom where it will rarely be seen or admired.

Circus Hoop

Stitch count	97h x 94w
Design size	17.5 x 17cm
	(7 x 6¾in)
Fabric	27-count Zweigart
	Linda evenweave
	in beige
	(or a 14-count Aida)

Follow the chart on page 131 of the Motif Library, working over two fabric threads (or one block of Aida), using two strands of stranded cotton for full and three-quarter cross stitches. Work French knots and backstitches with one strand. To embellish, push a piece of feather through a sequin and sew in place where marked on the chart. Use a beading needle and beige thread to sew on the beads and sequins under the clown's umbrella. Decorate the hoop and make up as described, right.

Mounting Work in a Hoop

Cross stitch embroidery can be mounted into a hoop, as shown by the circus scene on the previous page. The hoop can be edged with a trimming such as broderie anglaise or in the case of the circus hoop, bound with different coloured threads to echo the theme of the stitching. Small pieces of work can also be mounted in a flexi-hoop (see page 28).

Decorating the Circus Hoop

1 Bind the embroidery hoop to resemble the circus ring by first marking off 2.5cm (1in) segments with a pencil. Spread thin fast-tack glue over one segment at a time and wrap stranded cotton or other thread of your choice tightly around the hoop, ensuring that the wood is covered. Bind alternate segments in red and white. Make sure that all the thread ends are stuck down firmly.

2 Tack (baste) backing fabric to the wrong side of the embroidery to hide the back of the work. Position the lined embroidery face up, centrally over the inner hoop. Place the outer hoop over the embroidery and press down into place, with the screw adjuster at the top. Make sure the design is straight and then tighten the screw adjuster until the embroidery is evenly stretched.

3 Trim away excess fabric on the wrong side and glue down the raw edges on to the back of the inner hoop. Glue a length of narrow braid over the raw edges for a neat finish.

Mounting Work into Cards

Cross stitch embroidery is perfect for creating handmade greetings cards. You can use a simple single-fold card, where the embroidery is stuck to the front of the card, or use a double-fold card, which has a window or aperture for the design. If you want to avoid having to make your own card mount, use one of the many ready-made mounts that are available.

Mounting Work into a Single-Fold Card

Trim your embroidery to the size required leaving two or three extra rows all round if you want a fringe. Pull away the outer fabric threads to form the fringe and use double-sided tape to attach the embroidery to the front of your card.

Mounting Work into a Double-Fold Card

1 Buy your card mount first and ensure your embroidery will fit the card 'frame' before you start to design and sew. Lay the card right side up on top of the design so the stitching is in the middle of the aperture. Place a pin in each corner and remove the card. Trim the fabric to within about 1.5cm (⁵⁄₈in) so it fits into the card.

2 On the wrong side of the card, stick double-sided tape around the aperture and peel off the backing tape (some ready-made cards already have this tape in place). Place the card over the design, using the pins to guide it into position. Press down firmly so the fabric is stuck securely to the card. Remove the pins.

3 On the wrong side of the card, stick more double-sided tape around the edge of the middle section. Peel off the backing tape and fold the left section in to cover the back of the stitching, pressing down firmly.

Making Your Own Card Mount

If you opt to make your own card mount, you are free to produce a design of any shape or size you wish. Use thin card, which can be any colour you choose and can complement the embroidery. Before cutting the card make a quick, rough mock-up in paper to check that the card will fit the embroidery. The window can be any shape you require: rectangular, square, round, oval or heart-shaped but do not attempt to cut it out with scissors: for a professional finish, use a sharp craft knife to cut away the window opening. Use the back of a craft knife or a bone folder to score the fold lines. The instructions below will create a card with an aperture of about 5.6cm (2¼in) square but the measurements can be changed.

1 Choose a card colour to complement your embroidery and cut a piece 30 x 12cm (12 x 4¾in). On the wrong side of the card, draw two lines dividing it into three sections of 10cm (4in). Score gently along each line with the back of a craft knife or a bone folder to make folding easier.

2 In the centre section, mark an aperture slightly bigger than the finished size of the design – the diagram shows an aperture of 5.7cm (2¼in) square, with a border of about 2.2cm (⁷⁄₈in) along the top and sides. Cut out the aperture with a sharp craft knife, carefully cutting into the corners neatly. Trim the left edge of the first section by 2mm (¹⁄₈in) so that it lies flat when folded over to the inside of the card. This will cover the back of the stitching. Fold the left and then the right section on the scored lines. The card is now ready for your embroidery.

tip

For a neat edge that does not fray, fuse iron-on adhesive to the back of your embroidery and then trim the embroidery to size before fixing it to the front of your card.

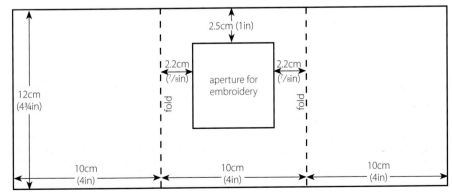

Fig 2 Making a double-fold aperture card

Making Up a Ring Pillow

The ring pillow on page 81 is quite simple to make up, and these general instructions could be used for any cushion or pillow.

You Will Need

- Linda fabric same size as the embroidered fabric
- 2.5m (2½yd) of 7.6cm (3in) wide cream lace edging
- 1.5m (1½yd) of 3.2cm (1¼in) wide eyelet lace
- 1.5m (1½yd) of 6mm (¼in) wide cream ribbon
- 1m (1yd) of 3mm (⅛in) wide cream ribbon
- 5.5m (5½yd) of 3mm (⅛in) wide apricot ribbon
- Seed beads in cream, pale green and pink
- Ribbon roses, four cream and two apricot
- White sewing thread
- Cushion pad 25.5cm (10in) square

1 When the embroidery is complete, place the two pieces of Linda fabric right sides together and seam together, allowing a 1.25cm (½in) seam allowance and leaving an opening in one side. Turn right side out, insert the cushion pad and slipstitch closed.

2 Sew the ends of the lace edging together and neaten the raw edges. Gather the lace into a frill, distribute all gathers evenly and sew it around the edge of the cover 2.5cm (1in) in from the seam line.

3 Thread thin cream ribbon and then wide apricot ribbon through the eyelet lace so that the apricot ribbon lies on top of the cream ribbon. Sew the eyelet lace over the edge of the lace frill to hide the gathered edge, mitring the corners so they lie flat. Sew a pink, green and cream bead at regular intervals along the ribbon line.

4 Make four multi-looped bows of apricot ribbon and sew one to each corner. Trim each bow by sewing on a cream ribbon rose.

5 Cut the wide cream ribbon in half, fold each piece in half and attach on each side of the pillow. Sew the apricot ribbon roses at the top on the folds of the cream ribbon.

6 Tie the wedding rings to the cream ribbons, and to stop them rolling around, hold them temporarily in place with pins.

tip
You may need a beading needle to sew on small seed beads, which is longer and thinner than a normal needle.

Making Up a Napkin Ring

A napkin ring is quick to sew, especially if you use one of the decorative initials on pages 36–43, and easy to make up. The napkin rings shown on page 38 were made from Hardanger fabric, with the initial stitched over two threads in the centre of a 10 x 15cm (4 x 6in) piece.

1 Once stitching is complete, press if required and then fold the fabric in half lengthways, right sides together.

2 Using a 6mm (¼in) seam allowance, seam the two long sides together, leaving a gap in the centre for turning through. Seam the two short sides (Fig 3).

tip
Hardanger fabric is ideal for creating napkin rings as it launders well.

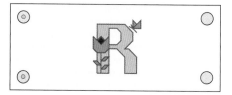

Fig 4 Attaching the press fasteners to the napkin ring

3 Turn the napkin ring the right way out, slipstitch the opening and press the seams. To finish, attach two press fasteners in the positions shown in Fig 4 above. The best press fasteners for the job are the kind that you hammer in, though the ordinary sewn-on variety is adequate.

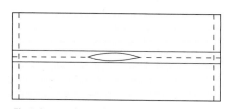

Fig 3 Sewing the napkin ring together

Covering an Album

The Family Album design on page 61 has been used to cover an album and makes a lovely keepsake. You will need an album which has pages on to which photographs are mounted, not the flip-up kind.

You Will Need

- Embroidery fabric to cover the album
- A photograph album
- Tacking (basting thread)
- Matching sewing thread

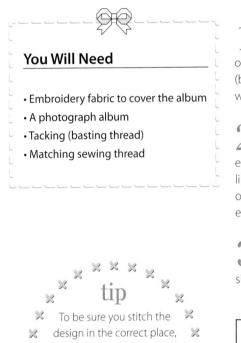

tip

To be sure you stitch the design in the correct place, tack (baste) an outline of the design on the fabric, removing all the tacking when the embroidery is finished.

1 Fold your fabric around your album and cut enough to allow for turnings on all sides and for two end pockets. Tack (baste) the fold lines and make a note of which section is to be embroidered (Fig 5).

2 If your album has a dark-coloured cover that will show through the embroidery fabric, it is best to use a lining fabric. Tack a similar sized piece of white cotton fabric to the back of the embroidery when stitching is complete.

3 Hemstitch the turnings on the inside of the cover. With wrong sides together, fold section A over B and slipstitch to form a pocket Fig 6). Repeat with the other end, folding section D over C, slipstitching to form another pocket. Remove all tacking. Slip the album cover into the two end pockets and smooth the cover in place.

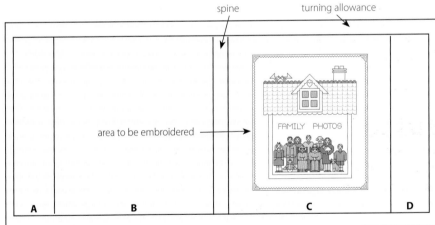

Fig 5 Layout of fabric to be cut for an album (right side)

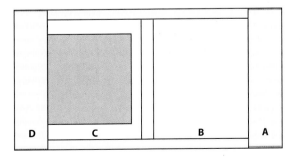

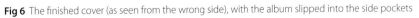

Fig 6 The finished cover (as seen from the wrong side), with the album slipped into the side pockets

Motif Library

This Motif Library is filled with hundreds of patterns, all designed for use on a mix-and-match basis and to add to the basic patterns given elsewhere in the book. Choose the motif you require, copy it out on to a separate piece of graph paper (or photocopy it) and incorporate it into your design. Small changes of detail will alter the patterns and make them more personal and versatile. A wide range of topics is covered, to allow you to make a comprehensive record of your life and stitch a huge variety of designs for samplers, cards, gifts and keepsakes.

If the motif you have chosen is facing in the wrong direction, hold a small hand mirror beside it and copy out the mirror image to reverse the direction. Alternatively, scan the motif into a computer and flip the image. All the motifs are in colour but no keys are given as you will probably want to change the colours to suit your own taste.

Family and Pets

The figures here can be changed to suit your needs by altering small details when you are copying them. To make figures taller, add a few squares to the length of the legs or torso, and to make them shorter, use fewer squares. In this way, children can be given different heights to indicate their ages. If you prefer grandparents standing, copy out the basic adult figure and add white hair, spectacles, or whatever features are needed to make them recognisable. Minor details on the uniforms for a Brownie, a Girl Guide, a Cub and a Scout can be changed to suit any troop. If you have an unusual pet, make a tracing of it from a book and square it up as described on page 18.

People

As this book is about a personal approach to design, people appear regularly throughout. The clothes we wear can often indicate the work we do, so one way of showing an occupation is to dress a figure appropriately. In some cases figures can also be shown using, or carrying, the tools of their trade. To create a brand new figure, draw out the basic figure and add the hat of your choice, the hair style, clothing and shoes from other figures. With a little ingenuity you can create any uniform you need. Small changes of detail, such as the addition of a beard or spectacles, can make your figure resemble the real-life model even more closely.

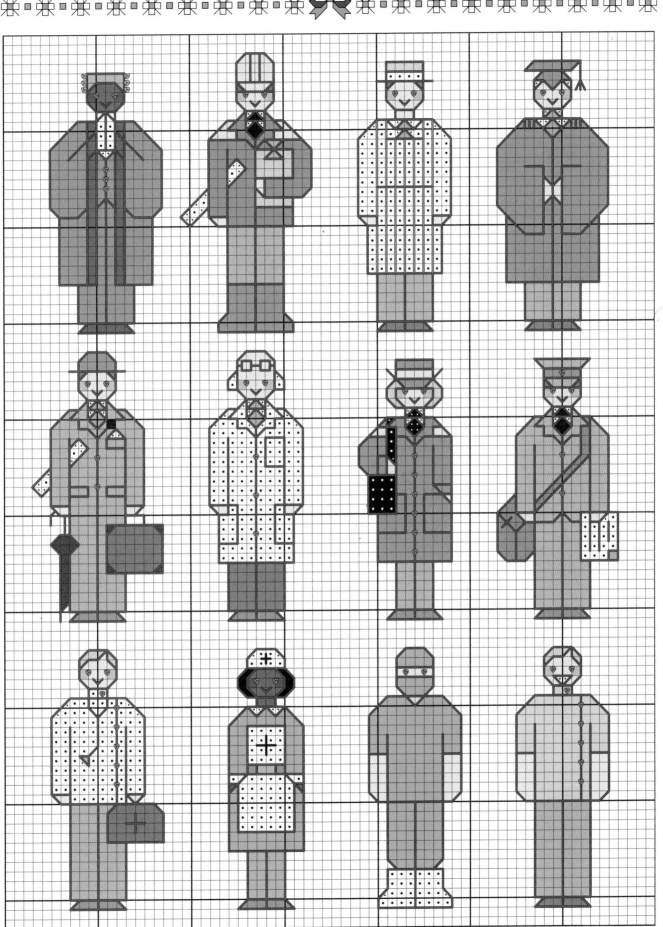

Occupations

If the occupation you wish to portray has no uniform or distinguishing clothing, you may be able to make use of the tools of the trade or the place of work. For example, a hammer and saw can represent a carpenter, and a magnifying glass over a £ or $ sign can represent an auditor. There are symbols to represent sales persons, computer operators, insurance brokers, business people, stockbrokers, typists, writers, telephonists, clerical workers, scientists, the medical profession, chemists, teachers, jewellers, weather forecasters, estate agents, photographers, film stars, politicians, the oil industry, garage owners, forecourt attendants, shopkeepers, shop assistants, film makers, draughtsmen, conjurers, locksmiths, security service personnel, electricians, geologists, factory workers or owners, mechanics, home handymen, carpenters, heating engineers, plumbers, and anyone with a certificate showing his or her qualifications. Most of the symbols provided here have more than one meaning, and hence more than one use. For example, the typewriter could be used by a typist or by a writer; and the blackboard can indicate what is taught if the lettering on the board is changed to suit the subject. If the occupation is in the leisure industry you may find what you want in the Home and Leisure or the Sport section. Even the Transport section on pages 122 and 123 can be of use, as the name of a firm or company can be backstitched on to the side of a van or a lorry.

Nationality

There are numerous ways to reflect nationality in your work, but perhaps the easiest
is to use a flag. Many flags are simple combinations of stripes, or consist of crosses,
neither of which should present many difficulties in designing for cross stitch.
National plants can be used: the English rose, the thistle of Scotland, the Welsh
leek and the Irish shamrock are given here. Native animals should not be
overlooked, hence the koala. For the musically inclined, you could use the National
Anthem, such as the first few bars of 'God Save the Queen' here.
Costume associated with a country can be colourful and need not necessarily be the official
national costume, for example the English morris dancer. The Scotsman is dressed in his kilt,
which can be sewn to suit any clan. Examples of figures of other nationalities are included, all
easy to identify. The seven-branched menorah candlestick can be used to represent Judaism.

Home and Leisure

This page will help you to represent work in the home and leisure activities. In fact, what is leisure to some, will be work to others, so many of the symbols here will have a double meaning. Thus the suitcase can represent leisure to a holiday maker, or work to a travel agent; and the ironing board represents sheer torture for me, but is a soothing pastime to others. Other leisure activities include camping (tent), photography (camera), painting (easel), flower arranging (vase), ballet (shoes), drama (masks), games (die), card games (ace), philately (stamps), poetry or sculpture (bust), reading (book), and a jigsaw piece for jigsaw addicts. The clock is for antique collectors or for clock repairers. The silver cup has been included for those who excel at their hobby and win prizes for it. Do not overlook organizations or clubs you may belong to or work for: many of these have badges suitable for squaring up into cross stitch patterns.

Cats and Dogs

Do not despair if your animal does not appear here. If you see a dog or cat as a combination of a head shape, plus an ear shape, a body shape and a tail, many more breeds can be produced by mixing the material here. Study your animal and alter the colouring to suit its personal characteristics. Experiment by putting different ears, tails or noses on different bodies. If this fails, get a picture of the breed and follow the tracing and squaring-up instructions on page 18. You will have less awkward curves to deal with if you show the dog seated facing you, or you could try a lying down pose. If you place your dog in a kennel, you will only have the face to contend with. If all else fails, represent your animal by means of a feeding bowl showing its name. If you wish to record the fact that your cat is a good hunter, include a mouse or two. Dogs in frames are useful where you do not have sufficient room to show the whole animal, or if the head is the only part you feel you have captured correctly.

Animals

Country dwellers, farmers, and those who work with animals or have unusual pets may want to include in their designs the animals they see each day. The shape and colour of the cow and the bull can be altered to produce other breeds. Equally, many breeds of pig are possible if the colouring is changed. The sheep is accompanied by a ram, which is just a basic sheep shape with added horns. The horse has been given a saddle, which can be easily removed, and the donkey has the distinctive dark cross on its back. Numerous birds are included. Animals, if repeated in lines, can be made into borders and bands. Suitable candidates for this treatment are the bees, mice, snails and ducklings. The frog fits neatly into a corner. Remember to make your animals face inwards and, where you have a long line of them, split the line in two and make each half face the centre; otherwise they will look as if they are about to walk, hop, fly or swim out of the picture. More exotic animals can be produced by the tracing and squaring-up method described on page 18. So, if you are the proud owner of anything from an aardvark to a zebra, all is not lost if your animal does not appear here.

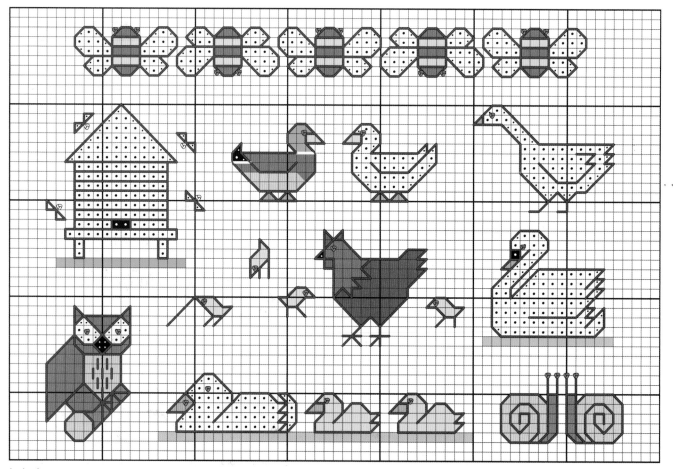

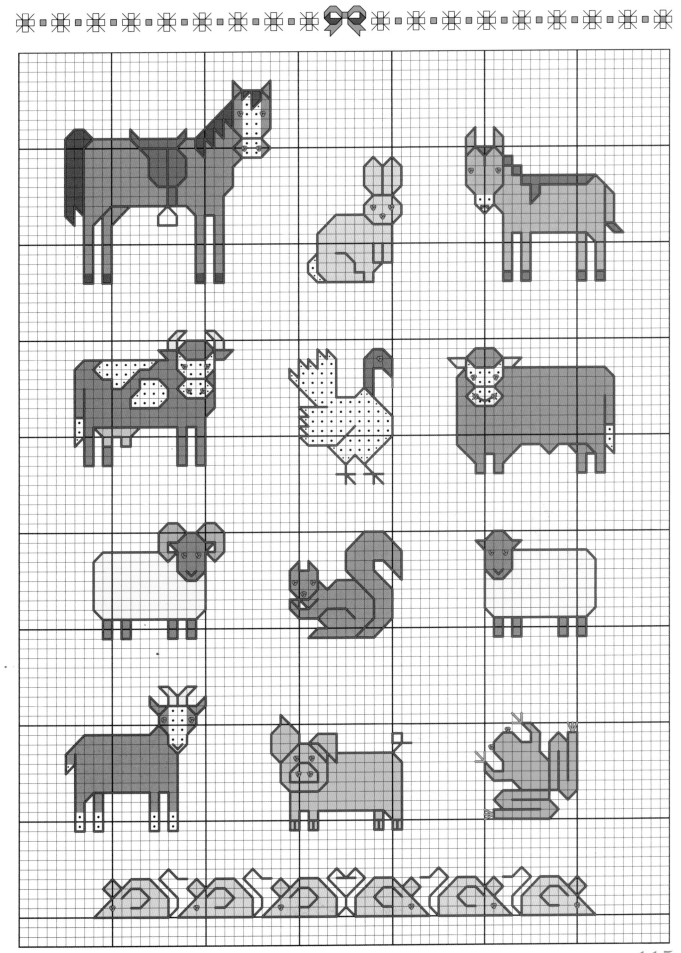

Sport

Once again the basic figures have been drawn out and this time the appropriate sportswear has been added. Any team strip can be produced by changing colours. If you want a younger player, reduce the height by shortening the legs. Children invariably play with one sock up and one down, so adjust the socks accordingly. The referee has adopted a characteristic pose and has a whistle in his mouth. For those who excel at their sport a medal can be placed around any neck or a figure can stand on a winner's rostrum. The golfer is in plus-fours to show off his brightly patterned socks, but he could be more casually dressed in golfing trousers and a peaked cap. If the sport you wish to represent has no special clothing to distinguish it, you may be able to make use of the equipment used in the sport, for example, the rifle to represent shooting. When sewing strings on to tennis or squash racquets, use a darning technique with one strand of thread. Lay the horizontal threads between the cross stitches on the top of the work and weave the vertical threads on and out of the horizontal threads. At the end of one string bring the thread through to the back and out again at the beginning of the next string. The darning lies on top of the fabric and looks quite realistic.

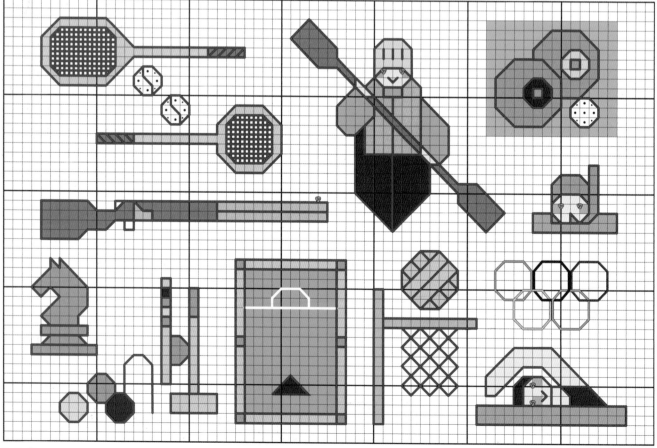

Gardening

Flowers appear here as single specimens and general flower shapes, all of which can be used to create borders of the sewn rather than the sown variety. See page 134 for borders. Some garden furniture and accessories have been included. The line of fencing can be extended to any length to form a band at the top or bottom of a design. For a gardening sampler, choose a border of flowers, butterflies or bees. Place an alphabet and numbers at the top and a gardening saying at the bottom. A gardener can be drawn by adding a gardening apron, gloves and watering can to one of the basic figures. Fill the remaining space with any of the patterns in this section.

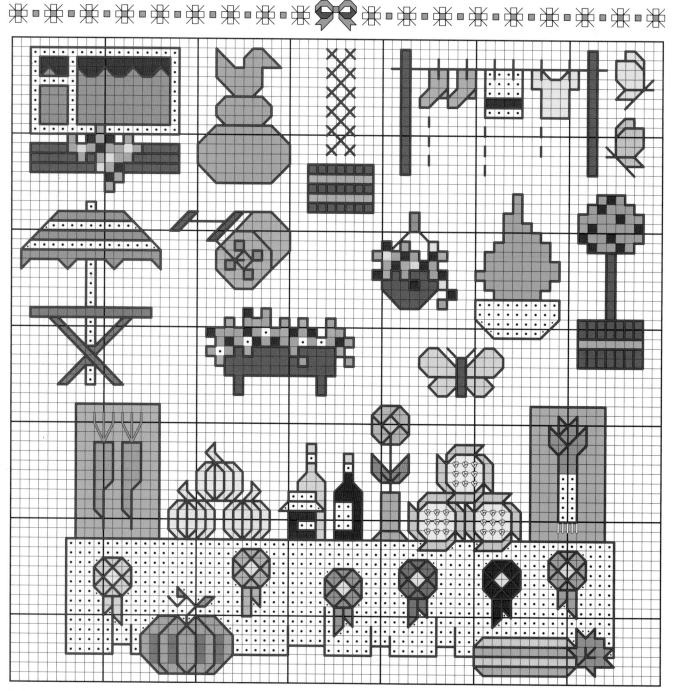

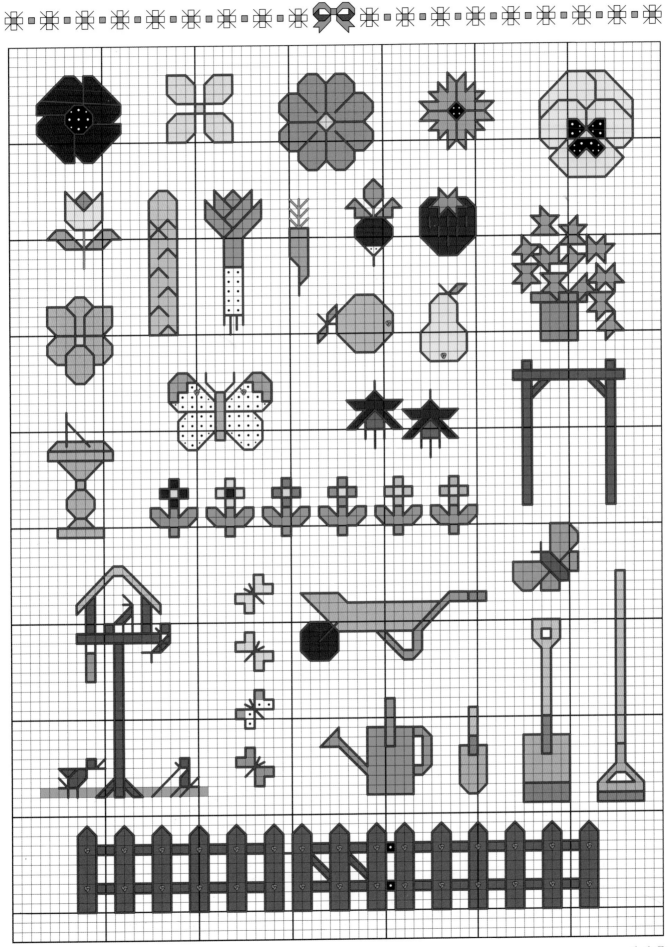

Music

A range of musical instruments is shown here. If sewing the bagpipes, choose your own tartan; embroider the basic squares and then add the fine lines of colour over the top in backstitch. The strings on musical instruments, their tuning pegs, keys, knobs and buttons, can all be added in backstitch and French knots.

Opera singing is represented by the performers. Two well-known opera heroines have been designed for you – Brünnhilde from Wagner's Ring Cycle and Carmen from Bizet's opera of the same name but using the basic figure and a little ingenuity, any role is possible. A choir boy represents choral singing or church music, but an adult version can be produced using a basic adult figure as your starting point. Gilbert and Sullivan lovers will recognise performers in *The Pirates of Penzance*, the *Yeomen of the Guard* and *The Gondoliers*. For characters in *The Mikado* see page 108, for *Trial by Jury* see page 103 and for *Madame Butterfly* see page 108.

Any bars of music can be drawn out quite accurately. Use backstitch to embroider the stave, and whole crosses for the notes if you have room; if not, use French knots.

Favourite tunes can be reproduced in their entirety if you have the patience, and can then be decorated with suitable designs and an appropriate border. See also page 109.

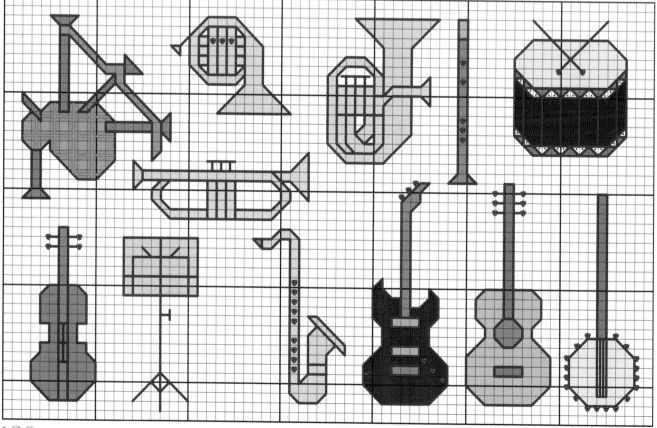

Transport

A general car shape can be adapted to resemble more closely the make of car you want. Racing cars appear in two sizes, and if the small one is placed behind the large one, it is possible to achieve the effect of a race in progress. One bus has been designed face on, a space-saving device which works well for many vehicles. The articulated lorry could have the name of a company written on the side, using backstitch. The bicycle can be adapted to a lady's model by removing the crossbar, and the drop handlebars can be replaced with upright ones. Sailing is represented by the small yacht and the ocean-going liner. If you are going to design a large sailing ship, make liberal use of backstitch for the rigging. A modern jet is given in two sizes, and a biplane for pioneering aviators. The hot-air balloon can be enlarged to accommodate any pattern or wording you may wish to add.

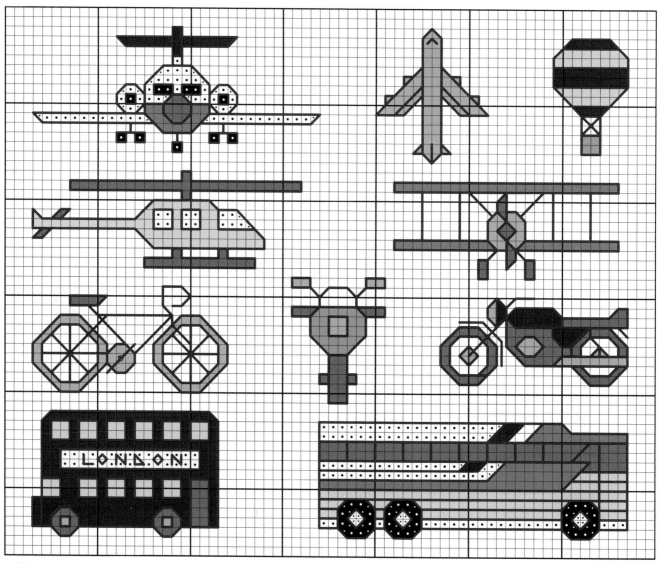

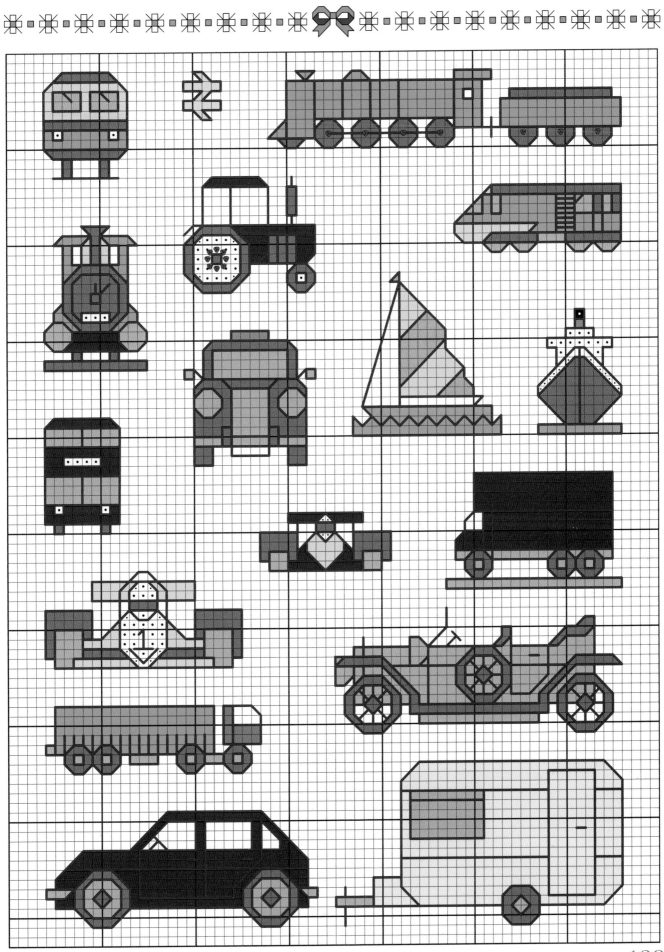

Houses

The houses and various architectural objects charted here may help you create a cross stitch embroidery of your home. If not, you can adapt these motifs to fit. See the detailed advice on page 56 on constructing your own house pattern.

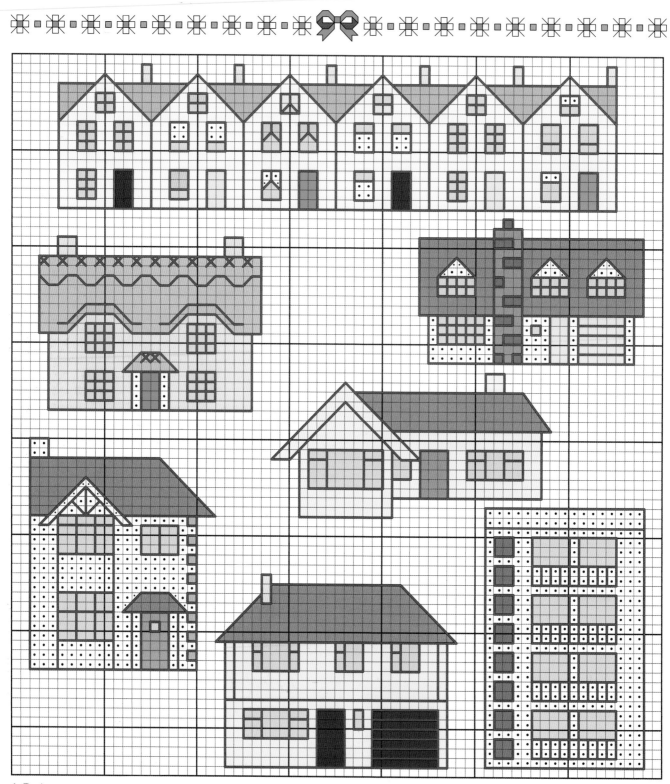

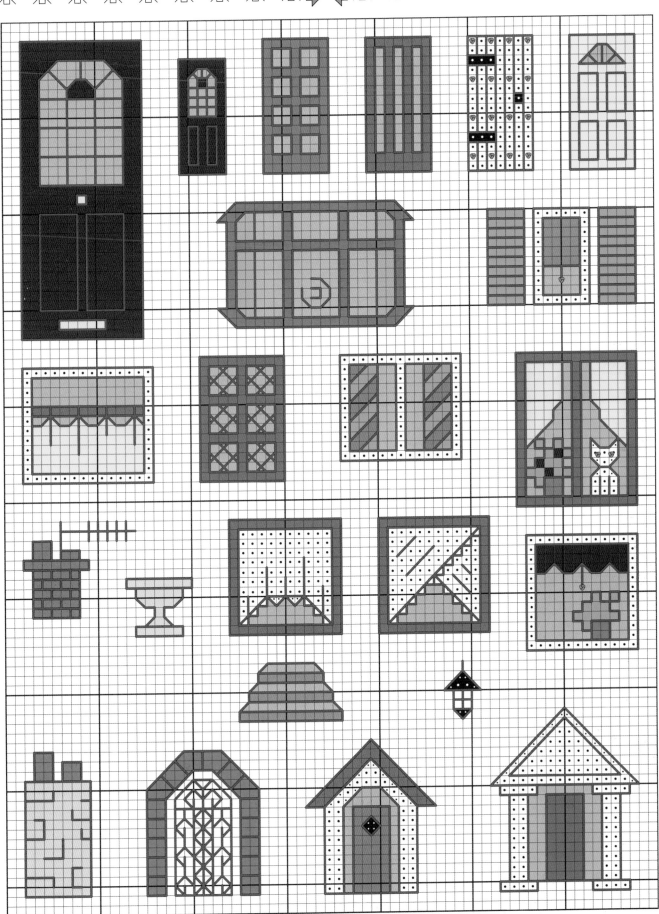

Christmas and Traditional Motifs

Some Christmas patterns have been included in this Motif Library, which can be used in samplers, for gifts and for greetings cards. You could also repeat motifs to create bands and borders. There are more seasonal motifs charted on page 42. You could also use these small motifs to decorate an alphabet, as described in the Decorated Initials chapter on pages 36–43. The traditional motifs shown opposite are useful when creating your own family tree sampler – see page 68 for further advice.

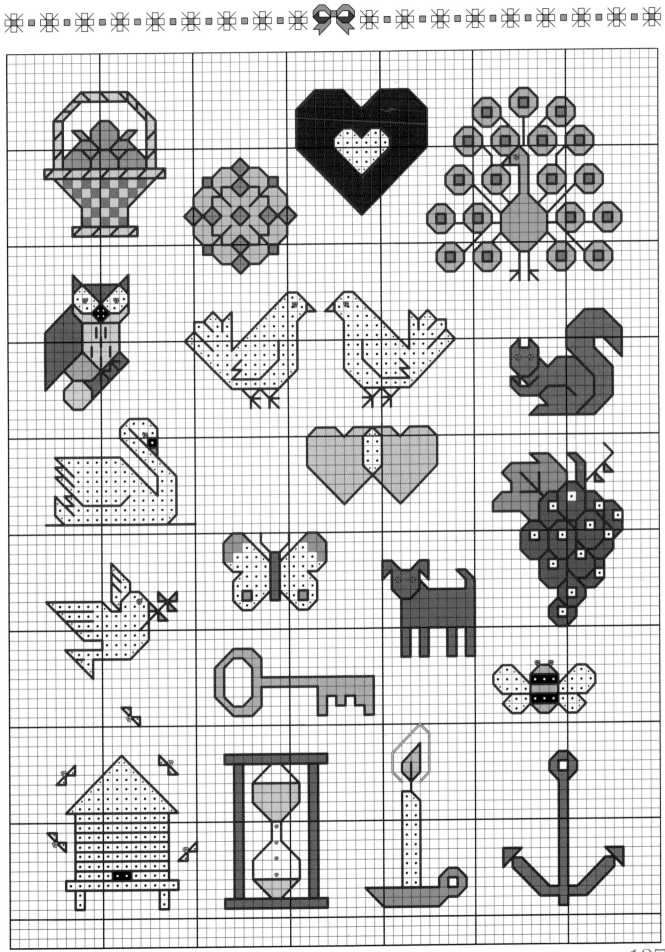

Weddings and Anniversaries

The wedding and anniversary motifs charted here are quite versatile and can be adapted to fit many occasions. The anniversary roundel is shown celebrating a 40th ruby wedding anniversary but the colours can be changed to suit another date and the number altered – for example, change the hearts and ribbon to blue and the number to 45 for a sapphire wedding anniversary. You can change the messages and dates using the alphabets, numbers and messages charted on pages 67 and 140–142. See also the Love and Marriage chapter beginning on page 78 for further advice and ideas.

Toys and Entertainment

The Birth and Babies chapter beginning on page 84 has advice on designs for children, in particular recording births and celebrating christenings. The motifs here will give you further ideas – perhaps you could use them for birthday cards or to decorate an initial or for a nursery sampler. The circus characters are shown on page 95, made up into a brightly coloured hoop.

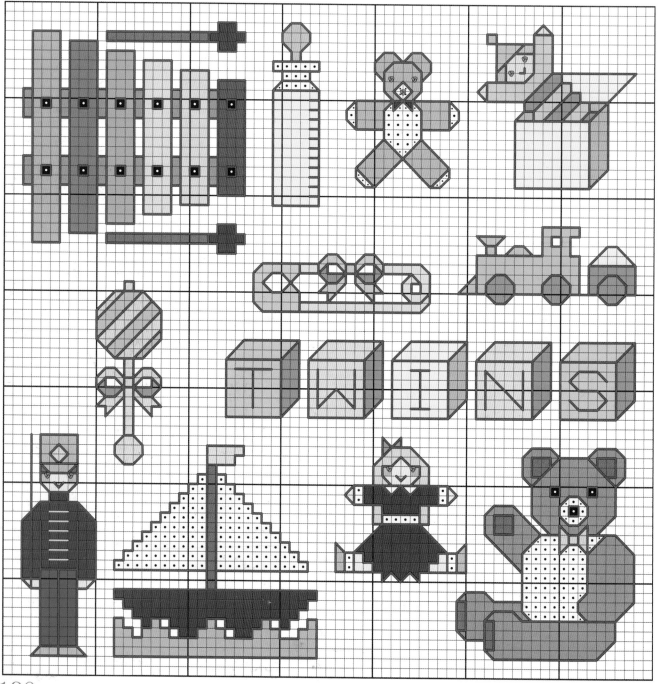

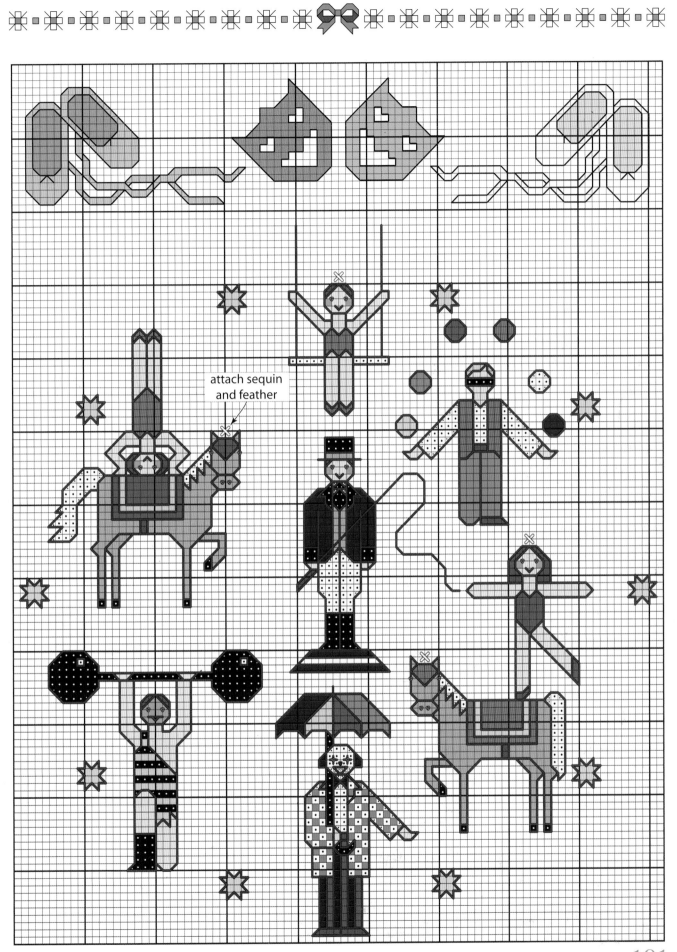

attach sequin
and feather

Mottoes and the Zodiac

Mottoes and sayings featured regularly and prominently on old samplers, where they tended to be of high moral tone and lugubrious nature. This was supposed to instruct the young needleworkers in the virtues of hard work, piety and filial obedience. For a contemporary embroidery, use a modern quotation, or even something humorous. Mottoes can be written out in the alphabet of your choice and inserted into your design, or they can be illustrated.

The four mottoes here are accompanied by an illustrative symbol. 'Post tenebras lux', meaning 'After darkness, light', is for optimists. When drawing a banner for your text, try to get the same amount of text on to each of the end pieces, so that they are the same length. The Girl Guide motto, 'Be Prepared', is placed above the Girl Guide badge. 'Per ardua ad astra', the motto of the Royal Air Force, which means 'Through struggles to the stars', has two stars in the text.

The signs of the zodiac are supplied as pictorial versions and as symbols – choose one or the other depending on the space you have available.

Pisces	Feb 20 – Mar 20	**Gemini**	May 22 – June 21	**Virgo**	Aug 24 – Sept 23	**Sagittarius**	Nov 23 – Dec 21
Aries	Mar 21 – Apr 20	**Cancer**	June 22 – July 23	**Libra**	Sept 24 – Oct 23	**Capricorn**	Dec 22 – Jan 20
Taurus	Apr 21 – May 21	**Leo**	July 24 – Aug 23	**Scorpio**	Oct 24 – Nov 22	**Aquarius**	Jan 21 – Feb 19

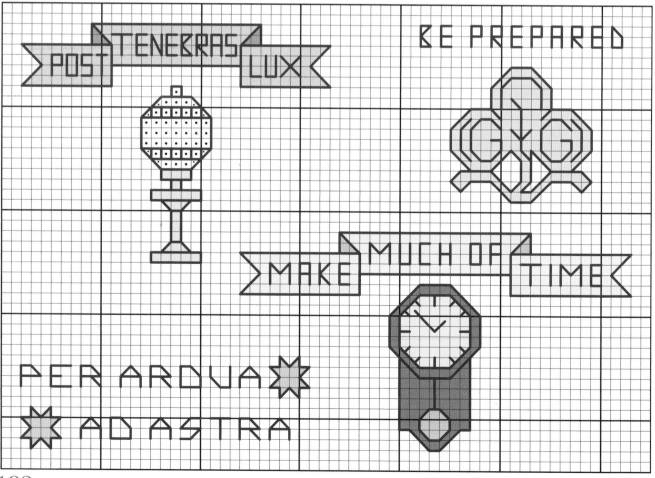

Bands, Borders, Fillers and Alphabets

The following pages contain a variety of useful designs that you can use to create your own embroideries or customize the charts in this book. There are also many alphabets, numbers and short messages to use. Some of the bands given here will need the addition of a corner to turn them into borders (see page 21). The borders can be lengthened or shortened to fit your design – add extra pattern repeats to lengthen, or remove the necessary number of repeats to shorten, as the case may be. Whatever border you choose or design, ask yourself if it would benefit from the addition of a retaining line. In some cases two lines on the outside and one on the inside can be effective. Experiment with coloured crayons and graph paper to make geometric borders if these are more to your taste, or play around on screen of you are using charting software. Throughout the book you will find borders surrounding designs but if none of these is suitable there are many small designs which can be repeated to create the border you require.

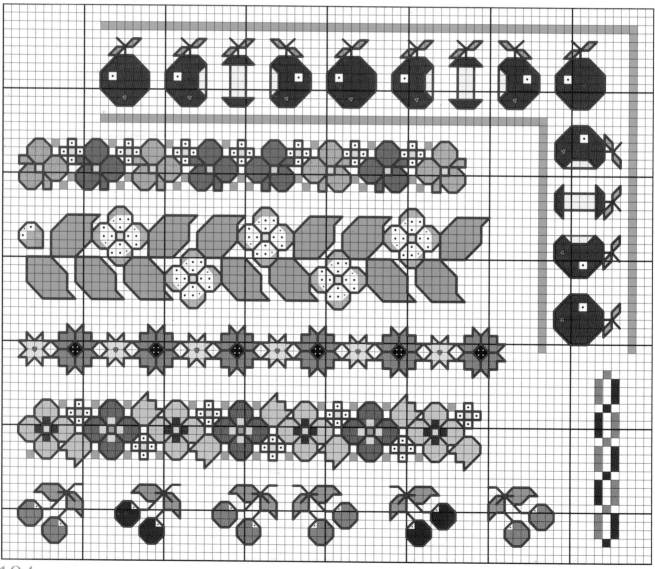

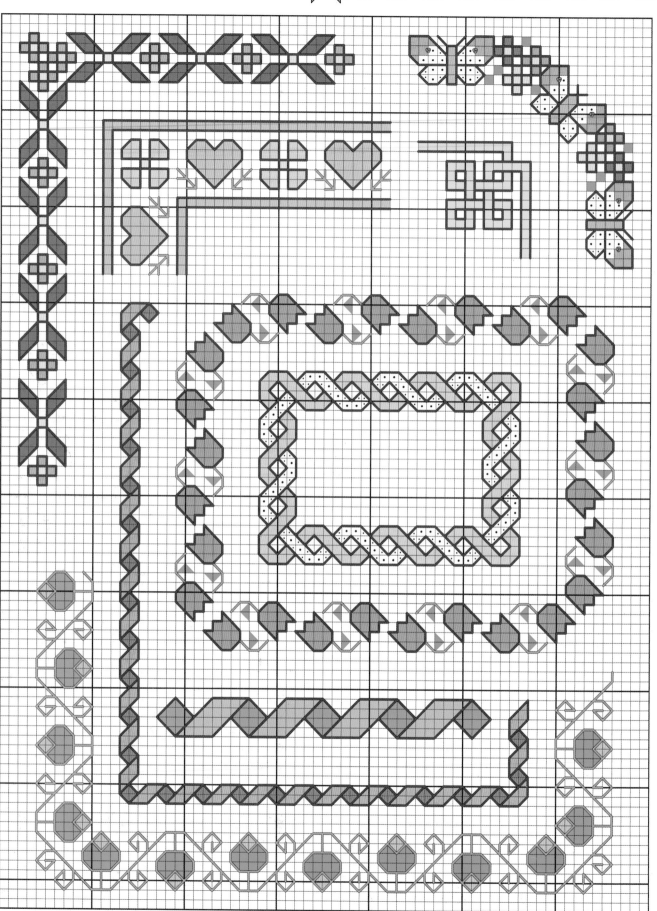

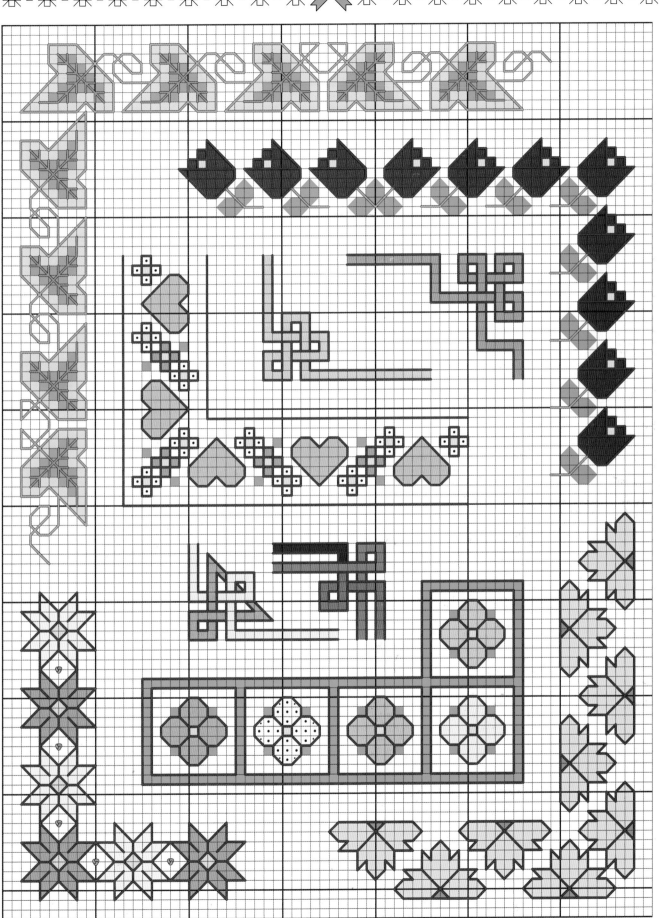

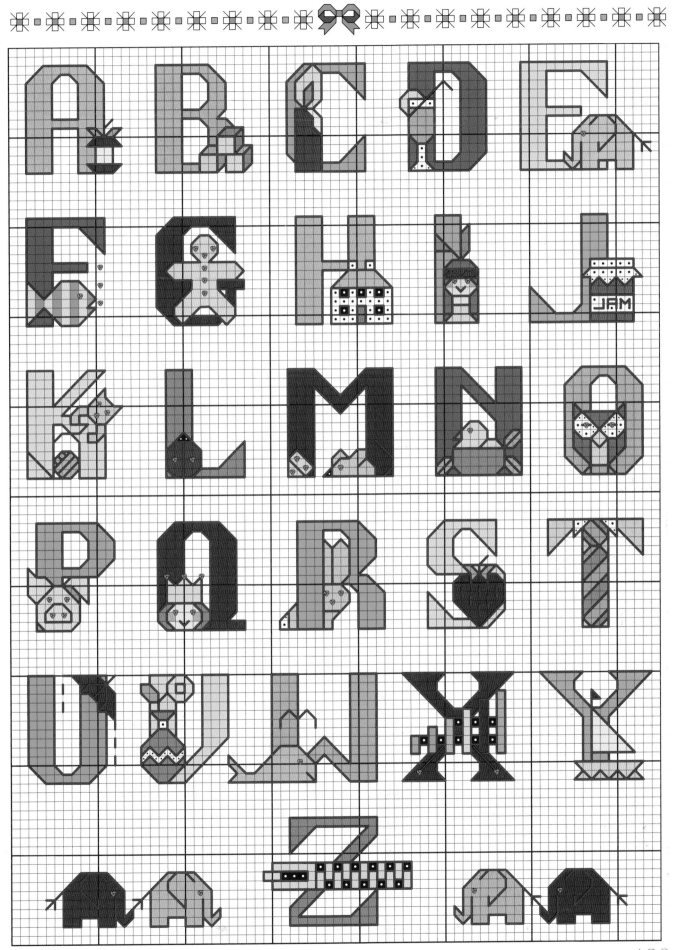

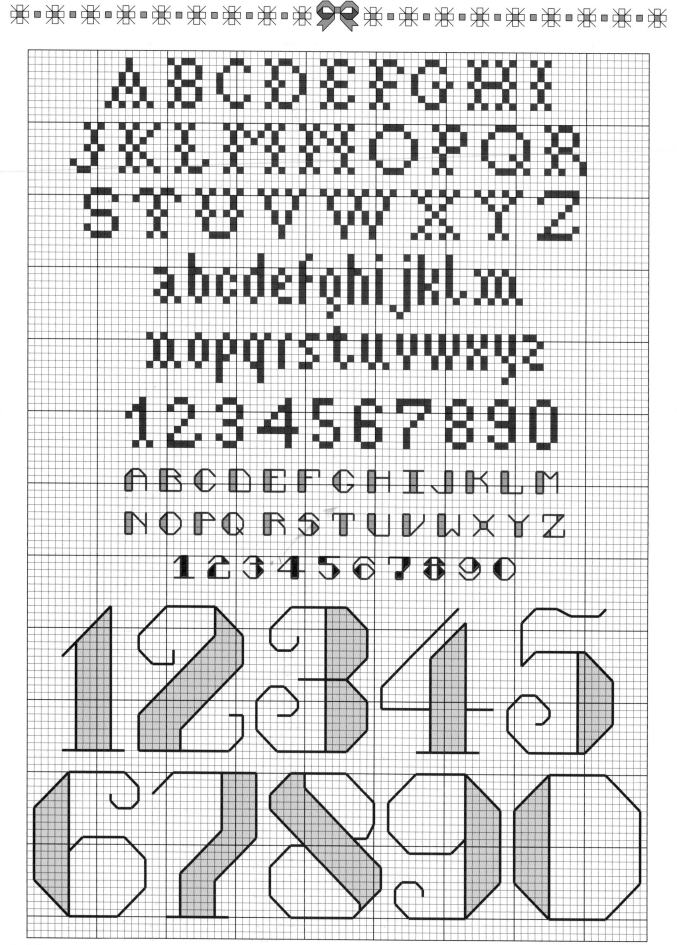

MOTHER   FATHER   BROTHER
SISTER   GRANNY   GRANDAD
UNCLE   AUNT   NEPHEW
NIECE   SON   DAUGHTER
TO DEAR   WITH LOVE FROM

THANK YOU   BEST WISHES
GOOD LUCK   FRIEND ♡ !?—

MERRY CHRISTMAS

HAPPY NEW YEAR

HAPPY ANNIVERSARY

HAPPY EASTER

♡
Congratulations!
♡

HAPPY BIRTHDAY

WELCOME !   NEW HOME

GET WELL SOON

WELL DONE !!   THANK YOU

House and Family
Sampler
(page 55)

Ring Pillow
(page 80)

Dove Card
(page 80)

You could use this
alphabet with any
of the upper case
alphabets in the
Decorated Initals
chapter, changing the
colour as desired

Suppliers

UK

If ringing from outside the UK use +44 and no (0)

Coats Crafts UK
PO Box 22, Lingfield House, McMullen Road, Darlington, County Durham DL1 1YQ
tel: 01325 394237 (consumer helpline)
www.coatscrafts.co.uk
For Anchor stranded cotton (floss) and other embroidery supplies

DMC Creative World
Pullman Road, Wigston, Leicestershire LE18 2DY
tel: 0116 281 1040
www.dmc.com
For stranded cotton (floss) and other embroidery supplies

Framecraft Miniatures Ltd
Unit 3, Isis House, Lindon Road, Brownhills, West Midlands WS8 7BW
tel/fax (UK): 01543 360842
tel (international): 44 1543 453154
www.framecraft.com
For items with cross stitch inserts

Heritage Stitchcraft
Redbrook Lane, Brereton, Rugeley, Staffordshire WS15 1QU
tel: +44 (0) 1889 575256
www.heritagestitchcraft.com
For Zweigart fabrics

Madeira Threads (UK) Ltd
PO Box 6, Thirsk, North Yorkshire YO7 3YX
tel: 01845 524880
email: info@madeira.co.uk
www.madeira.co.uk
For Madeira threads

Willow Fabrics
95 Town Lane, Mobberly, Cheshire WA16 7HH
tel: 0800 056 7811
www.willowfabrics.com
For fabrics and bands, beads and threads

USA

Charles Craft Inc.
PO Box 1049, Laurenburg, NC 28353
tel: 910 844 3521
www.charlescraft.com
For fabrics and pre-finished items

Kreinik Manufacturing Company, Inc
3106 Timanus Lane, Suite 101, Baltimore, MD 21244
tel: 1800 537 2166
email: kreinik@kreinik.com
www.kreinik.com
For metallic threads, blending filaments and silk threads

MCG Textiles
13845 Magnolia Avenue, Chino, CA 91710
tel: 909 591-6351
www.mcgtextiles.com
For cross stitch fabrics and pre-finished items

Mill Hill,
a division of Wichelt Imports Inc.
N162 Hwy 35, Stoddard WI 54658
tel: 608 788 4600
www.millhill.com
For Mill Hill beads and a US source for Framecraft products

Yarn Tree Designs
PO Box 724, Ames, Iowa 500100724
tel: 1 800 247 3952
www.yarntree.com
For cross stitch supplies and card mounts

Zweigart/Joan Toggit Ltd
262 Old Brunswick Road, Suite E, Piscataway, NJ 08854-3756
tel: 732 562 8888
www.zweigart.com
For cross stitch fabrics and pre-finished table linens

The Cross Stitch Guild

The Cross Stitch Guild was formed in 1996 and quickly became a worldwide organization with a committed and enthusiastic body of members, with cross stitch and counted thread addicts around the world delighted to have a Guild of their own. Members receive a full-colour magazine, *Stitch That* with Jane Greenoff, including free counted cross stitch designs and technical advice and information. The CSG also supplies cross stitch tours, weekends, cross stitch kits, gold-plated needles, stitchers' gifts and counted thread classes. Taster Membership and Full Membership is available and there is a website with discounted shopping.
www.thecrossstitchguild.com
For more information or for the latest catalogue contact Jane Greenoff: CSG HQ, Pinks Barn, London Road, Fairford, Gloucestershire, GL7 4AR UK. Tel (from UK) 0800 328 9750; (from overseas) +44 1285 713799.

Acknowledgments

The author's thanks go to Helen Fairchild for her encouragement, without which this book might not have been written. Thanks also go to Mr J. Edwards and Mrs L. Sheen for permission to reproduce 'Apple End'.

Thanks are due to the many stitchers who produced work for this book, including:
Gill Broad (Amy Christmas Stocking), Carol Burr (Summer Garden Sampler), Sylvia Morgan (Tree of Knowledge Sampler, Apple Family Tree, Gather Ye Rosebuds, Nancy's Milestones, Circus Hoop), Val Morgan (18th Birthday Display Case), Elizabeth Smith (Amy door plate), Linda Smith (Birth Announcement) and Irene Vincent (Winter Garden Sampler).

The author's estate also wishes to thank Lin Clements and Cheryl Brown (David & Charles), The Nimble Thimble (Rugby), Iris Woolcraft Centre (Leamington Spa), Coats Crafts UK, Cara Ackerman (DMC Creative World), Wembly Graphics (Wembly), Tony Foster (Warwick Studios) for framing, and Ethan Danielson for the charts.

Index